THE
LAND
OF
OSIRIS

THE LAND OF OSIRIS:

AN INTRODUCTION TO KHEMITOLOGY

STEPHEN S. MEHLER

ADVENTURES UNLIMITED PRESS

CONTENTS

....

PART ONE: KHEMITOLOGY

PART TWO: THE LAND OF OSIRIS

PART THREE:
BRINGING IT ALL BACK HOME

DEDICATION

....

To Estelle Muriel and Philip,
whose love is the reason I am.

To Theresa Louise, whose love and support
is the reason this book was accomplished.

And to Abd'El Hakim, whose love and
wisdom lives in these pages.

LIST OF FIGURES

··

Chapter Eleven

Chapter Twelve

ACKNOWLEDGMENTS

....

I HAVE ALWAYS BEEN AMUSED watching the Academy Awards presentations and seeing the recipients rattle off a long list of people to thank for helping them to achieve the award. I have often felt the same reading the long lists in acknowledgment pages in the books I have read. Now that it is my turn to do so, since this book represents over 30 years of research and work, I can deeply sympathize with the desire of others to give credit and recognition to everyone who has helped along the way.

First and foremost, the greatest thanks and appreciation goes to my life partner, Theresa Louise Crater, not only for her love and emotional support, but for spending many hours discussing and editing the preliminary drafts of the manuscript. Without her help, energy and patience with my stubbornness in my writing style, this book would never have been possible.

The support of my family and friends enabled me to endure the many travails and obstacles in the decades of dedication to this effort. My brother Bob Mehler and sister-in-law Sunny Goldstein Mehler have always been in my corner and have helped in so many ways, as has dear family friend Layne Hackett. Thanks to Joni, Rick, Steve and Kristine Mehler for patiently listening to their uncle's radical ideas and ravings for so many years. I am also very grateful for the love and support of Ron and Phyllis Hoffman and Max and Raquel. Special thanks must be extended to Sol and Frieda Kalski Goldstein for their parent-like love and encouragement for over 30 years.

There are so many people who have influenced me and provided inspiration for this journey. Thanks to Dr. Margaret Conkey for the introduction to archaeology and prehistory, Dr. H. Thomas Harvey for instilling in me a love of natural systems and holism, Professor François Bordes for the initial field training and experience in archaeology, Dr. George F. Buletza for teaching me to be both a scientist and mystic, and to Dr. Albert H. Doss for his spiritual guidance and encouragement. I must also mention John Anthony West for his inspiration as a great independent researcher and Egyptologist, author Murry Hope for her encouragement and support in my path of research, and Zecharia Sitchin for his scholarly research example.

There are so many dear friends who have aided me both personally and professionally: Francoise Beaudoin, Julia Jordan Catlin, Diane Hardy and Shawn Levin, Josephine Stuart, Porkey Lewis and the whole extended Lewis-Pounds families, Gary Mitchell, Joani Hoffman, Anne Shrage, Eddie and Georgette Gale, Guy Dickinson, Shasta Bates, Paul Rader, Tom Rogers, Daniel Schmidt, Wendy Allen, Cherie and Hank Bersok, all the many Rosicrucians who helped me, Beth Hedva, Mary Seaira, Ralph Martin, Susanne Gilen and Ravi, Olga Peck, Jan Blair and Elizabeth Lamar, Steve Ferchaud, Ama Fox, Bobbie and Larry Wright, Jim Cyr, Joe and Marylee Swanson, Ruth Adele and Susan Earnhart, William Stephenson, Tom Krupa and Tom Hunt. My thanks to anyone I might have left out.

Special love and thanks goes to Wilma Faye Moore. Faye has been a second mother to me and has provided great love, support and spiritual guidance for many years.

Those who have played a direct role in aiding in the research and support for this work include: Bonnie McKenzie and John Morais, Robert Vawter and Helen Lund, Ed Heft, Willis Winters, Dr. A. J. McDonald, Paul Bowman, Chuck Putnam, Christopher and Jeanne Dunn, Dr. John DeSalvo, Charles Jacob, Dr. Toby and Theresa Weiss, Harry and Dr. Ruth Hover, Jeff Rense, Laura Lee, Hilly Rose, Doug Kenyon, Harry Osoff, Carl Hart, Bob and Teri Brown, Gary Hardin, Paul Tice and Tedd St. Rain, Dr. Chet and Kallista Snow, F.R "Nick" and Khrys Nocerino, Sandra Bowen, JoAnn and Carl Parks and Max the Crystal Skull, Flordemayo, Mary Thunder, Aluna Joy Yaxk'in, Mac McCrary, Ehrton and Naomi, Robert Mitchell, Karena and Ronnie Bryan and especially, Rodney Birkett for his friendship and beautiful art work for the cover.

I must also deeply thank Barbara Hand Clow for initially providing encouragement, help and advice with the early manuscript and ideas and for her inspiration as a great teacher, Jon Graham for his support, Joan Parisi Wilcox for her valuable suggestions, and Riki Mathews for copy-editing the final version. Special thanks to John Rutter of the Image Department of the National Geographic Society, Kurt Wehrberger of the Ulm Museum, Germany, and extra special gratitude and thanks to Renata Tyree of Executive Solutions for final design, layout and preparation of the book. My deepest appreciation and thanks to David Hatcher Childress for his great role model as a world traveler and researcher, and as owner of Adventures Unlimited Press for publishing this book.

The final and greatest thanks is to Abd'El Hakim Awyan, and his family, without whose knowledge, wisdom and trust this book could never have been what it is.

INTRODUCTION

·······································

WHEN WE ALL REACH a certain state of maturity in our lives, it is a natural recourse to look back at past events and remember certain instances that either changed the course of our lives or made a profound impact on us. For me, a significant event occurred around the age of eight. My mother, bless her memory, always kept around our house two great pictorial magazines, *Life* and *National Geographic*.

I clearly remember thumbing through a copy of *National Geographic* and stopping dead on a page with a photograph of the Sphinx and Great Pyramid of Giza, Egypt. I stared at the photograph for a long time, and although I could not consciously articulate what was happening to me at that time, I know now a profound connection was created within the depths of my being. The Sphinx awakened something within, and from that day to the last day of this life, I have been and will be fascinated by and drawn to anything concerning ancient Egypt.

In the last ten years, I have been fortunate to have gone to Egypt several times and have never failed to pay respect and homage to the Sphinx as soon as I arrive. The Sphinx is the Guardian of all Egyptian Mysteries, and for many centuries her secrets were veiled to most humans. But an ancient prophesy is now at hand, and the veil is slowly being lifted for those who wish to know.

In 1992, a miraculous series of events led me to a narrow street in the village that nestles next to the Giza Plateau. In a house with a great view of the Sphinx lives a man who, almost single-handedly, has brought forth an ancient tradition to lift that veil. His name is Abd'El Hakim Awyan, recognized Elder and Indigenous Wisdom Keeper of an oral tradition that extends back tens of thousands of years. In the countless hours spent around the shisha water-pipe with innumerable cups of tea, a tradition was unfolded before me, a tradition decidedly African in its style and exposition. To think of Egypt as part of the Middle East would be incorrect as Egypt is part of Africa, and the teachings I was exposed to are most definitely part of the living African oral tradition.

The great mystic George Gurdjieff once posed a question that I have paraphrased and stated in three parts: namely, is there a purpose to life, is there a purpose to human life in particular, and is there a specific purpose to our individual lives?[1] Gurdjieff maintained every thinking human being had to address these thoughts sometime in their lives. I feel now that the Sphinx stimulated me with the mystery of those questions at a tender age and unconsciously set me on the path to discover for myself some answers.

This book is the result of my life-long search for those answers. For over 30 years I have been formally researching information about ancient Egypt, but it is essentially my almost fifty-year search for my own personal origins that has led me to the oral traditions of ancient Africa and to the great wisdom of that most venerable birthplace of all humanity.

The indigenous teachings presented in this book are consistent with a trend that occurred around the globe in the later half of the twentieth century and is continuing into the twenty-first. On all continents of the Earth, indigenous wisdom keepers have been stepping forward and presenting oral histories that have long been kept in small, tight circles of initiates. All these teachers have been indicating it is time to present these stories, that a great cycle is coming to an end, and it is necessary to tell all people the indigenous wisdom and knowledge in preparation for the coming changes. It is in this spirit that I will present what has been taught to me as a framework to better understand where we have come from, our true origins, to enable us all to better deal with what is coming.

The uniqueness of the teachings in this book are reflective of the style of teaching of Abd'El Hakim. Utilizing both sides of the brain, Abd'El Hakim presents the physical evidence—archaeological, geological and philological—to satisfy the left brain, the scientific, rational mind yet also evokes the right-brain's holistic, experiential process of receiving knowledge directly into one's being. In that light, I will offer scientific evidence gathered in the field along with pictures and a narrative of personal events to present the teaching that an advanced civilization existed in Northern Africa well over 10,000 years ago. This civilization, known as ancient Khemit (not Egypt), composed of indigenous tribes rather than culturally superior outsiders (whether called Atlanteans or extraterrestrials), was possessed of sophisticated knowledge and wisdom, and these were the people who created the Sphinx and Pyramids we see standing today.

These ancient Africans known as Khemitians built the structures called pyramids for the generation, transformation, utilization and transmission of energy, most certainly not as tombs for kings. Of all the contemporary theories about the construction of the Great Pyramid, the ideas of master craftsman and engineer Christopher Dunn come closest to the ancient Khemitian tradition. In his book *The Giza Power Plant*, Dunn presents the concept that the Great Pyramid was built as a machine to produce energy. One of the major sources of this energy was water, the profound understanding of which was known to the ancient Khemitians and has only recently been rediscovered in the last hundred years by men of genius like Viktor Schauberger and Johann Grander.

Abd'El Hakim introduced to me a concept of a geographical area he called *Bu Wizzer*. Translated as *The Land of Osiris*, this was a part of ancient Khemit that stretched from the present sites of Dahshur in the south, to Abu Roash in the north and included the well known areas of Sakkara and Giza. Covering approximately 25 square miles, these sites all had pyramids and temples constructed on them and a myriad of underground tunnels made by the ancient people in order to bring water to the area. The indigenous tradition that Hakim represents teaches that these sites, known collectively as *Bu Wizzer*, were active living places well over 10,000 years ago.

The accepted paradigms and concepts of Egyptology are in need of major revision. As a background for this approach, I will utilize the ideas of Professor Thomas S. Kuhn, who first coined the phrase "paradigm shift" in the 1950s. As a graduate student in the 1970s, I was greatly influenced by Kuhn's book *The Structure of Scientific Revolutions.* In this book, Kuhn proposed the radical concept that the real changes in science occur dramatically in a revolutionary fashion, not gradually. I hope to ferment the seeds of revolution with the new paradigms presented in this book.

It would be foolish to propose or suggest that this one book will topple the entire discipline of Egyptology. The primary goal here is to present a new set of ideas and paradigms, an entirely new way to interpret and experience the magic that was ancient Egypt. But even more so, the intent will be to stimulate and provoke young minds, even old minds, to question and observe in perhaps a different way than we have been taught in the West. I wish to help people to realize that we have always been more than we have been taught we are, that we have enormous potential as creative, multi-functional and multi-dimensional beings, to see that all existence is holistically interdependent and interrelated as indigenous people do.

My experiences on this path and my journey to this point have led me to know that the people we now call the ancient Khemitians had a wisdom and understanding that has indeed endured through thousands of years of darkness. This wisdom and understanding, exemplified by people like Abd'El Hakim, is now being offered to all people in divine timing for the coming great shift in consciousness that is humanity's destiny.

PART ONE:

KHEMITOLOGY

CHAPTER ONE

THE JOURNEY BEGINS

 SCIENTISTS ARE USUALLY taught to leave themselves out of their work as science purports to be an objective reporting of the facts. But the latest findings in quantum physics have demonstrated that the thoughts and feelings of the observer affect the observed. Our own consciousness interacts with what we study and influences the outcome. For this reason I feel it is pertinent to start with some history of my own personal journey to this point in time. I feel it is necessary in this case to present a proper framework for the reader to realize how these conclusions, theories and ideas have been arrived at.

This idea of presenting one's individual history or journey, though quite popular in the West, is quite antithetical to Eastern, Native American and other indigenous traditions. My own Egyptian teacher, Abd'El Hakim Awyan,[1] considers it quite embarrassing to dwell on his own life; however, I think the evolution of ideas and theories, and why certain concepts are accepted and others rejected, may be sometimes as important as the ideas and theories themselves.

It would be incorrect to say that after I connected to the Sphinx at a young age I became determined that either ancient history, archaeology or Egyptology was to become my life's goal—nothing so dramatic happened—but I did develop a deep interest in anything Egyptian. However, the only information presented to me in my youth on the subject was our well known story of Exodus in the Old Testament of the Bible surrounding the Jewish holiday of Passover. In this version of history the Egyptians were depicted as cruel taskmasters, enslaving the Hebrews and receiving the wrath of God for their efforts. But soon after the experience of making my unconscious connection to ancient Egypt, I began to seriously question this presentation. What I received (although, again, I could not articulate what that was at this age) from staring at pictures of the Sphinx, Great Pyramid and anything ancient Egyptian did not equate with a cruel and oppressive people cursed by God.

So in my early teen years I rejected religion as a system for learning any objective truths. I became intensely interested in science, almost all the sciences, as being the path to discover the truths I sought. My academic career was then oriented to some achievement in science, although not yet leaning toward anthropology, archaeology or Egyptology. I enjoyed biology, chemistry, physics and all the natural sciences. As an undergraduate I majored in chemistry but switched to human physiology and anatomy when advanced mathematics and calculus proved to be my downfall. At 21 years of age, I graduated college with a BA in physiology and anatomy, with a minor in chemistry, and with a strong desire to engage in some sort of medical research in order to contribute to a great discovery that could help humanity rid itself of diseases.

I attempted to go on to graduate school to further my goals, but when those plans did not work out, I enlisted for four years in the US Air Force. This was in 1967, and the United States was involved in the Vietnam conflict. Needless to say, those four years changed my life. Besides explorations into alternate states of consciousness, I used that time to delve into areas of literature I hadn't had time for in my college years.

In the process of indulging in works of Eastern religion, mysticism and metaphysics, one particular book made an overwhelming impact on me. As an undergraduate I had always maintained an interest in the work of Sigmund Freud. In 1968, I discovered his "last works" in a used paperback entitled *Moses and Monotheism*, first published in 1939. Having been interested in the history of Judaism before, I was astounded to learn Freud's claim that Moses had been an Egyptian priest, and the Mosaic teachings came basically from an Egyptian king named Akhenaten. Freud had written a series of essays for the psychoanalytic journal *Imago* in Vienna, Austria, in 1937 and 1938, postulating that the Hebrew lawgiver Moses had been a priest of the Egyptian King Akhenaten, and it was the teachings of monotheism as promoted by this Egyptian king that Moses taught to the Hebrews and that became the basis for Mosaic Judaism.[2] In early 1939, Freud fled the Nazis and settled in London where he wrote a third essay before he died, and the three essays were published posthumously in late 1939 as the book *Moses and Monotheism*.

This book did indeed change the direction of my life. I became fascinated with this king Akhenaten; I read everything I could find about him, beginning my own education in Egyptology by reading the works of Petrie, Breasted, Gardiner, Aldred, Maspero, Budge, Murray and many others. After getting out of the Air Force, I settled in California to pursue graduate work in the natural sciences. I had developed an interest in ecology because of its holistic approach, the realization that everything in nature is interconnected and interdependent. Although I pursued my own research in Egyptology, my thoughts for a career were in the environmental fields. While working on an MA in the natural sciences, I took a class entitled "Prehistoric Man and His Environment" in 1973, taught by Dr. Meg Fritz (who has since returned to her maiden name, Margaret Conkey, and currently teaches at the University of California, Berkeley). Meg became a personal friend as well as mentor and instilled in me a love and passion for archaeology. She arranged for me to work on an archaeological dig in the summer of 1974.

It was on this excavation in the south of France that I met and worked for Professor Francois Bordes of the University of Bordeaux, then

Director of Antiquities for southwestern France. Professor Bordes, whose background and doctorate was in geology, taught me not only field archaeology but basic geology as well. After this, there was no turning back for me; I was "hooked" on prehistory and archaeology, with a primary interest in Egyptology. I continued extensive research on my own.

I returned to San Jose State University in 1977, where I had received my first master's degree, to continue my academic pursuits. Working through the Social Sciences Department under the auspices of the Women's Studies Department (which is now defunct), I designed my own master's program in Egyptology, specializing in the role and position of women in ancient Egypt. I was greatly influenced by the works of such authors as Margaret Murray, Barbara Lesko and Merlin Stone in uncovering the matrilineal/matriarchal nature of the social structure in ancient Egypt.

In 1975, discovering Peter Tompkins' book *Secrets of the Great Pyramid,* I began intensive investigation into all the literature concerning the Great Pyramid. It was Tompkins' great holistic treatment of the subject that led me to seriously consider non-academic sources beyond the realm of Egyptology. In 1977, I got involved with the Rosicrucian Order, AMORC, in San Jose, California, and delved deeply into the metaphysical traditions about ancient Egypt as espoused by the Rosicrucians, Freemasons, and the Theosophical Society. I became more and more convinced that authors such as H. Spencer Lewis, Manly P. Hall, Rudolph Steiner and H. P. Blavatsky had inherited a tradition of metaphysics and mysticism that began or had much of its origins in ancient Egypt.

While working for the Rosicrucian Order as a Staff Research Scientist from 1978-1980, several significant events occurred. After having rejected religion and academia as sources for the answers I sought, I found a home in this metaphysical path. I accepted the fact that I was both a scientist and a mystic, and that not only were these two labels not mutually exclusive, but that many of the great scientists of the past, such as Plato, Sir Francis Bacon, Sir Isaac Newton, Robert Fludd, Giordano

Bruno, Johannes Kepler, Benjamin Franklin, Nikola Tesla and Albert Einstein, had also been deeply interested in mysticism. I realized that to understand what the civilization of ancient Egypt was truly about meant integrating science and mysticism, and this remains my approach today. I was led by the Director of the Research Department of the Rosicrucian Order, Dr. George F. Buletza, then one of the world's authorities on the neurophysiology of the brain and central nervous system, to the works of R. A. Schwaller de Lubicz, a French alchemist, mathematician and hermetic philosopher who founded the Symbolist School of Egyptology. Schwaller's research had convinced him that what Egyptology labels the civilization of ancient Egypt, called dynastic Egypt, was the recipient of the wisdom and knowledge of a much older, more profound civilization.

This was in 1979, and I then discovered the works of independent Egyptologist and author John Anthony West, in particular his book *Serpent in the Sky*. West is the most outstanding proponent and follower of Schwaller's work, and this book is the best introduction to his ideas. It was in this book that West first brought forth Schwaller's theory that the Sphinx was eroded by water, not wind and sand, and therefore was much older than the proposed date of 2500 BC as accepted by Egyptologists.[3] This idea has resulted in West's work with Boston University geologist, Dr. Robert M. Schoch, in re-dating the age of the Sphinx and the type of erosion evident.

Later that year I was approached by Hank Bersok, then an officer of the Grand Lodge of the Rosicrucian Order, and asked if I had ever heard the name Dr. J. O. Kinnaman. I replied I had not, and he gave me a cassette tape to listen to which was a recording of a lecture by Dr. Kinnaman in the mid 1950s to a small group of people in northern California (a group of people I later learned were all Masons). In this lecture Kinnaman mentions he had known Sir William Flinders Petrie, the great British archaeologist and the person considered to be the founder of modern Egyptology, for over 45 years and had worked with him in Egypt for over 11 years. Kinnaman claimed to have worked with Petrie in the Great Pyramid for many years. In this lecture Kinnaman begins with a normal, factual discussion of the Great Pyramid, i.e., how many blocks it contains, the estimated weights, interior chambers, etc. But later in the lecture Kinnaman casually mentions that he and Sir Flinders found a secret entrance into the pyramid on the south face (the "normal" entrance we all use today is on the north face) and discovered many other rooms and chambers not known to most researchers. Kinnaman claimed he and Petrie also found ancient "records" from Atlantis and "anti-gravitational machines" that had been used to build the Great Pyramid.

Needless to say, this tape knocked me for a loop! I listened to it over and over again. It became apparent that there were only three possible conclusions to be reached about Kinnaman's claims: either he was completely insane, a pathological liar, or there had to be some shred of truth therein. In my investigation into the matter, I discovered that Kinnaman had set up a foundation for research located in Lodi, California before he had passed away. I contacted Dr. Albert J. McDonald, Executive Director and President of the Kinnaman Foundation, and arranged a meeting with him in early 1980. I found Dr. McDonald to be an unassuming man, then in his mid 60s, utterly dedicated to the memory of Dr. Kinnaman, and convinced that Kinnaman was neither insane nor a liar. However, he could offer no proof to back Kinnaman's claims, but he did offer access to the Foundation's archives to follow up on investigations to prove (or disprove) Kinnaman (*see* Figure 1).

Although I was fascinated with Kinnaman's claims and my own continued research had led me to be open to the possibility of his alleged finds, I let the matter sit for a few years as I pursued other areas. I formed a collaboration with Robert M. Vawter, an acoustical and recording engineer, musician, and anthropologist, that resulted in our establishing The Monuments of Giza Research Project in 1989. The project was originally intended to investigate all possible sources of information concerning the Sphinx and Pyramids of Giza, Egypt. It has since expanded to the major theories presented in this book and is now called The Land Of Osiris Research Project and Bob Vawter has gone on to pursue other research interests.

Figure 1.
Dr. J. O.
Kinnaman,
early 1950s.
Photo cour-
tesy of the
Kinnaman
Foundation.

In the course of our research together, I shared with Bob the cassette and material I had gathered on Dr. Kinnaman. Bob then reconnected with Dr. McDonald, and we began an intensive investigation into Dr. Kinnaman's life. Originally called the Kinnaman Foundation for Biblical and Archaeological Research when formed in 1960, the title has now been shortened to simply the Kinnaman Foundation. I served as Director of Research for the Kinnaman Foundation from 1994-1999 when irreconcilable philosophical differences between Dr. McDonald and myself concerning the way the Foundation should present its findings prompted me to resign from the organization.

During the 1990s, Bob Vawter and I delved deeper into the literature with the works of Schwaller, Hall, Edgar Cayce, West and Blavatsky. We became convinced through these works, and especially with G. R. S. Mead's Theosophical book *Thrice Greatest Hermes*, that there had indeed been an inner group of adepts, masters and initiates who had directed the course of ancient Egypt and had inherited their wisdom and knowledge from an even more ancient civilization. These people were known in various sources as the Inner Temple, the Hermetic Brotherhood of Luxor, the Master of the Hidden Places, the Brotherhood of Tat, the Brotherhood of the Snake, or just simply the Brotherhood. We also entertained the hope that remnants of this tradition might still exist in Egypt, and it became our fervent desire to connect with members of this tradition.

The events that enabled this connection to be made were significant. I discovered the works of occult author Murry Hope, a Wiccan Priestess and student of the classical mystical tradition, who wrote the book *Ancient Egypt: The Sirius Connection* in 1990. In this book she mentions that she had connected with a group in Egypt that still held to an ancient tradition. She called this group the Ammonite Foundation and declared they had never been converted to Islam or Coptic Christianity and held traditions that could be traced back at least 3,000 years.[4] This was the first indication to me that this tradition still existed in present day Egypt.

An important event transpired in March of 1992. I attended a meeting with Bob Vawter that included Dr. McDonald and other members of the Kinnaman Foundation. This meeting was specifically arranged to confer with a man I had met years earlier (1979) when I was working for the Rosicrucian Order. The gentleman in question was Dr. Albert H. Doss, a psychiatrist practicing in North Carolina (now retired), a native born Egyptian from a prominent family and a high ranking Rosicrucian (*see* Figure 2). Among many other things, we discussed with Dr. Doss our belief that the Greek concept of Hermes Trismegistus (Thrice Greatest Hermes) symbolically represented three stages this mysterious brotherhood had gone through in Egyptian history. The different stages had been necessary as the members of this tradition had to go "underground" to protect themselves as their knowledge was being suppressed by the mainstream religious leaders. He agreed with us, and with his eyes closed, replied, "Yes, but there is a fourth Hermes." Bob and I immediately locked eyes and nodded, coming to the exact same conclusion: Dr. Doss

Figure 2.
Dr. Albert H. Doss (left) and author.
1992. Photo by Robert M. Vawter.

was confirming to us that the tradition still existed in Egypt. He later said he did not know of the Ammonite Foundation, but urged us to go find the living tradition for ourselves in Egypt. If it hadn't been before, it was now imperative that continuing this line of research required at least one, if not many trips to Egypt as soon as possible.

Through the aid of friends supporting the research, I was able to go to Egypt in November 1992. I went with a tour company called Power Places Tours run by some people I had met a few years earlier, Dr. Toby and Theresa Weiss. Toby and I had become acquainted at a San Francisco Whole Life Expo in 1987 and become friendly because we were both followers of the teachings of R. A. Schwaller de Lubicz. Along with this tour group was a subgroup led by author and teacher Nicki Scully, who was conducting initiation rituals at sacred Egyptian sites. I joined Nicki's group and was able to experience much with her as well as do my own investigations. The first day in Egypt I met the Egyptian tour guide used then by both Power Places Tours and Nicki Scully, Abd'El Hakim Awyan, known simply to everyone as Hakim (*see* Figure 3). He was well known as an Egyptian Egyptologist and had been a tour guide for over 40 years. It has now become very significant to me that the first time I ever saw Hakim he was standing in front of the Sphinx. I remember staring at him, then at the Sphinx, and then back at him. The Sphinx seemed to indicate to me that this man was someone I should pay close attention to. Certain remarks he made during our tour of sites and at the Cairo Museum led me to surmise that Hakim was not a Muslim, especially when he made the statement that he had been taught "by masters," and I felt he might be aware of the tradition I was seeking. Without hesitation,

Figure 3.
From left to right, Dr. Toby Weiss, Owner and Director of Power Places Tours, Abd'El Hakim Awyan, and author and teacher Barbara Hand Clow. 1992. Photo by author.

I pulled him aside in the museum and asked him if he knew of the Ammonites. He looked at me and replied that he did. I then asked him if he was one, and he grabbed both my hands in his, looked deeper into my eyes and replied, "Yes, how did you know?" I told him I had read Murry Hope's book, and he answered, "Ah yes, Murry!" I knew I had found the one I had been searching for!

Thus began an amazing relationship/tutelage with this remarkable man. I have since learned that he does not use the term "Ammonite" for reasons I will make clearer later, but prefers to be known as a Keeper of the indigenous traditions of the ancient culture called Khemit, not Egypt. An equally amazing thing is that he had not (in 1992) revealed himself publicly as an elder and wisdom keeper but was only known as an Egyptian Egyptologist and tour guide. Not even Dr. Toby Weiss, John Anthony West, nor Nicki Scully were aware of his "true identity" then although all used his services as tour guide. Only teacher and author Barbara Hand Clow recognized this "hidden" side of Hakim and did initiation tours with him from 1992-1996. Barbara has since stated to me that Hakim did reveal himself to her in December 1992 as a "Keeper of the Keys," in effect telling her that he was a wisdom keeper. To this day, Hakim will point to some of the guardians (those who maintain the ancient sites) and call them "Keepers" to let us know these people are part of his tradition.

During my first trip to Egypt and after the early discussions with Hakim, it became apparent to me that with the confidence and power with which he spoke of ancient Egypt, he was indeed privy to some esoteric information that had only been revealed in fragments before this time. Hakim confidently remarked that the Sphinx was well over 50,000 years old and that the major pyramids were considerably older and constructed for different purposes than Egyptologists had recognized. He also maintained that the middle pyramid at Giza, known as Khafra, was older than the Great Pyramid, and the first true pyramid constructed. Throughout our initial discussions Hakim left the door open for me to engage in deeper explorations into his knowledge. I came back from

Egypt in December 1992 with my head literally swimming with ideas and concepts to contemplate.

After that, I began to publish some articles with my preliminary research results. As a result, a series of synchronistic events led me to the work of master craftsman and engineer Christopher Dunn and his theories of advanced machining in ancient Egypt. I was privileged to be included in and to review an advanced copy of his great book *The Giza Power Plant*. As Dunn states in his book, he became interested in theories concerning the Great Pyramid in the 1970s. Trips to Egypt to do field work convinced Dunn that the Great Pyramid, due to the precision of its workpersonship and materials used, was designed to function as a machine, not as a tomb for a king. This analysis dovetails perfectly with the indigenous traditions as being taught by Abd'El Hakim.

It was from this point onward that the preliminary journey and stages of my life began to crystallize into the original research that is the focus of this book.

THE RESEARCH UNFOLDS

 **M**Y FASCINATION WITH anything ancient Egyptian and my preliminary research convinced me that all human origins, the beginnings of civilization, technology, spirituality and religion, had connections to very ancient Africa. The science of physical anthropology had put human origins in Africa, and the mystical tradition taught by the Rosicrucians, Masons and others had promoted the idea that all spiritual and metaphysical practices had their beginnings in ancient Egypt. As the last decade of the twentieth century progressed, three main parameters emerged for the foundation of my "new" approach to Egyptology: the work and claims of Dr. J. O. Kinnaman, the teachings of Abd'El Hakim Awyan and the theories of Christopher Dunn. The interrelated threads between all three pieces became more evident the deeper I delved into the research.

The problem then was to develop a coherent hypothesis as to why the accepted theories of Egyptology and anthropology were inadequate to explain humanity's, and the culture of ancient Egypt's origins, and to present a viable alternative set of paradigms based on a coalescence of the three parameters mentioned above. This would, of course, mean many more trips to Egypt and further investigations of alternative ideas.

In the first half of the decade of the 1990s Bob Vawter and myself decided to delve deeper into the claims and life history of Dr. J. O. Kinnaman and the Kinnaman Foundation. After having existed in several different permutations, the J. O. Kinnaman Foundation for Biblical and Archaeological Research was founded in California in March of 1961 for the purpose of investigating archaeological information as it pertains to the Bible and other historical sources (*see* Figure 4). As I investigated the writings and claims of Dr. Kinnaman I concluded that he might have been connected to the indigenous tradition due to certain statements he

Figure 4.
Dr. J. O. Kinnaman (left) and Sidney Foster of the Kinnaman Foundation. Late 1950s. Photo courtesy of the Kinnaman Foundation.

had made in his private lectures. Kinnaman had indicated he and Petrie had discovered documents that placed the age of construction of the Great Pyramid at over 36,000 years ago. In my first discussions with Hakim, he had stated the main pyramids at Giza were over 10,000 years old.

The research into the claims and life of Dr. J. O. Kinnaman in the last ten years has revealed some very interesting things. With four subsequent trips to Egypt in 1997, 1998, and two in 1999, I have yet to "find" a secret entrance on the south face of the Great Pyramid even though I found notes written by Dr. Kinnaman in 1995 pinpointing the "exact" location on the southwest corner. I have not found chambers or rooms in the pyramid with records from Atlantis nor devices used to build the structure by use of anti-gravity. However, I do believe certain devices have been found, some on display in the Cairo Museum (*see* Figure 5), that may be what Kinnaman was describing. A series of plates, made of the volcanic stone schist, may have been used to create a sound vibration to overcome gravity and enable the huge blocks of the pyramid to be placed so precisely. Levitation by use of sound is not a phenomenon recognized

Figure 5.
Cairo Museum. Plate made out
of volcanic schist stone. 1998.
Photo by author.

as valid by orthodox science but one mentioned in the metaphysical literature for centuries. Hakim has also consistently stated that sound played an important role in both cutting the hard stones and overcoming gravity to lift the stones in place.

Certain of Kinnaman's claims can be verified and certain others remain a mystery. Kinnaman's degrees are indeed legitimate; he graduated from Tri-state College in Angola, Indiana, in 1894, majoring in classical courses, specializing in Greek and Latin literature, ancient history, philology and classical archaeology. He did graduate work in Greek and classical archaeology at the University of Chicago for three years, starting

Figure 6. Dr. J. O. Kinnaman's doctoral degree. Courtesy of the Kinnaman Foundation. Photo by Robert M. Vawter, 1992.

in 1900. He received a Ph.D. in archaeology from the University of Rome in 1907, having associated himself with such famous Italian archaeologists as Dr. Cecre Gionetti and Dr. Rudolfo Lanciani (*see* Figure 6). We can document that Dr. Kinnaman was a Fellow and Vice President of the Victoria Institute of Great Britain, Vice President of the Society for the Study of the Apocrypha, a member of the International Society of Archaeologists, and the editor of five different archaeological magazines including being editor in chief of the *American Antiquarian and Oriental Journal*.[1] He was also editor of his own *Biblical and Archaeological Digest* and author of hundreds of articles and four books. The mystery that remains is that I cannot verify for certain his alleged relationship with Sir William Flinders Petrie.

In Petrie's autobiography *Seventy Years in Archaeology*, written in 1932, there is no mention of Kinnaman's name. In the definitive biography of Petrie, *Flinders Petrie: A Life in Archaeology*, written by a student of his, Margaret Drower in 1985, there is also no mention of Kinnaman. I wrote to Ms. Drower in 1992, and she confirmed she had never heard of Kinnaman nor seen any mention of his name in Petrie's notes, diaries nor in the Petrie archives in London. Correspondence with Ms. Rosalynn Jansson, assistant curator of the Petrie Museum in London, also confirmed no mention of Kinnaman in the archives of the Petrie Museum. So how can there be no evidence of an alleged 45 year relationship in any of Petrie's letters, diaries or notes on record? Nor did we find any letters from Petrie to Kinnaman in the Kinnaman Foundation archives in the five years I served as Director of Research.

The speculation arose that Petrie and Kinnaman might have been Masons, and loyalty to that organization may have prevented any disclosure of their friendship. Having a knowledge of Rosicrucian history, I knew that many famous individuals in the past had kept their associations with mystical organizations secret from the public, oftentimes even from their own family. In the Kinnaman Foundation archives, I did find evidence that Kinnaman was a 32nd degree Mason, and I am still trying to verify if Petrie was also a member. In many recently published books, such as *The Hiram Key* by former Masons Christopher Knight and Robert Lomas, certain Masonic rituals have been revealed to be directly derived from the initiatory practices of ancient Egypt. Although I do not agree with many of the conclusions drawn in their book, Knight and Lomas have done much to show the unbroken tradition of ritual from ancient Egypt to the modern metaphysical groups and that the Masons may have been more knowledgeable about ancient Egypt than many Egyptologists.

Kinnaman stated that no record of their finds in the Great Pyramid was established because he and Petrie both swore an oath to the governments of Egypt and Great Britain not to divulge in their lifetimes what they found. Kinnaman further stated that at the time of their discovery (which may have been in 1922), it had been decided by all concerned that the general populace was not ready to know about anti-gravity and the discoveries they made in the Great Pyramid. Interestingly enough, other researchers, such as Nikola Tesla and Viktor Schauberger, were also working on theories of anti-gravity at this approximate time period.

If such an oath were made, Sir Flinders certainly kept his word, as there is no mention of Kinnaman or of finding anything unusual in the Great Pyramid in any of his known writings or utterances. For his part, in his public lectures and books, Kinnaman only mentioned knowing Petrie but never mentioned any findings or anything out of the ordinary beyond the accepted facts about the Great Pyramid.

Towards the end of his life, however, in the mid-1950s (he died in 1961), Kinnaman gave some private lectures to groups of Masons. The tape I had heard in 1979 was recorded around 1955 in a private home in Stockton, California. It was in these lectures that he neglected his previous oaths and made his claims of secret rooms, chambers, records and devices found in the Great Pyramid. Was the alleged Masonic connection between Petrie and Kinnaman a primary reason there are no known records of their friendship, collaboration or finds?

There are some tantalizing bits of information that link Kinnaman and Petrie, if not directly, then indirectly. Besides both possibly being

Masons in the early decades of the twentieth century, they both were members of the Palestine Exploration Fund of Great Britain, the Victoria Institute of Great Britain (in the same years), and two colleagues of Petrie, Henry Offord and Joseph Proctor, regularly contributed articles to the *American Antiquarian and Oriental Journal* when Kinnaman was editor-in-chief (1911-1914). According to Petrie's autobiography, the only time he returned to the Giza Plateau to do research after his initial work in the 1880s and 1890s (Kinnaman claimed he first met him in 1894) was in March-April 1922, and I cannot verify Kinnaman's whereabouts during that time. Also, Dr. Rudolfo Lanciani is listed on Kinnaman's doctoral degree from the University of Rome in 1907 and is mentioned in Petrie's autobiography as a close friend, Sir Flinders and Lady Petrie often staying as guests in the Lanciani Villa during Petrie's many visits to Italy.

The few people who knew Kinnaman personally that we interviewed (some of whom have since passed away) steadfastly stated he was not a charlatan, liar or one given to tall tales. Ms. Willi Semple, a Rosicrucian who knew Dr. Kinnaman closely for the last six years of his life, wrote an article about him for the July 1962 issue of the *Rosicrucian Digest*. In it she stated, "How do I know it [the Great Pyramid finds] was a true story? For many reasons, but chiefly because it was impossible to know Dr. Kinnaman very long without also knowing, beyond doubt, that he would never lie or rationalize or imagine or even theorize about what might or might not be so, especially if it involved archaeology—he was a digger for facts, not a theorist."[2] Ms. Semple passed away in 1977, so she is not available for an interview, but her written words live on. Dr. McDonald first met Dr. Kinnaman in Denver, Colorado in 1945 and was very close with him for the last 15 years of his life. To this day, Dr. McDonald strongly believes that Kinnaman told the truth and staunchly defends his name.

There are other reasons for my continued interest in Kinnaman's declarations. Many of the things Kinnaman claimed to have discovered in the Great Pyramid fit very well into our current ideas of the age, function and methods of construction I propose. Kinnaman also claimed the face of the Sphinx was that of a woman, not a man.[3] As far as I know, Kinnaman was the only degreed archaeologist to have made this claim. I have also made this point in print, and it is important as regards the matriarchal/matrilineal nature of ancient Egypt. Kinnaman also used some translations of the hieroglyphic symbols and statements about the great antiquity of civilization in Africa that indicated he may have had contact with indigenous wisdom keepers.

In the last few years my major concentration of the research has been on the indigenous traditions still living in Egypt. This phase began in 1996 as Bob Vawter undertook a research trip to Egypt and met with Abd'El Hakim himself. Bob spent three weeks in the field with Hakim and was introduced to some of the teachings I present in this book. Later we met with Hakim in Alameda, California, in August of 1997 and engaged in intensive discussion of the indigenous traditions and teachings

Figure 7. Abd'El Hakim Awyan, at his home in the village of Nazlet el Samman, Giza, Egypt. 1997. Photo by author.

Hakim had decided to make public. We prepared for another research expedition to Egypt that took place in September 1997 (*see* Figure 7). The extensive field work I did with Hakim at that time enabled me to contemplate previously excavated material and evidence in a new way, in light of the indigenous teaching Hakim had presented to me. It became clear to me with each subsequent trip to Egypt and in continued discussions with Hakim that there was a coherent system of thought in the indigenous tradition he presented, a system of thought quite similar to other teachings evident in the writings of other researchers such as Carlos Castaneda, Gregg Braden and John Major Jenkins delving into indigenous wisdom. Coupled with the phenomenon of indigenous wisdom keepers emerging as public teachers, such as Hunbatz Men of the Maya Tradition and Thomas Banyanca of the Hopi Tradition, Hakim's "going public" with his indigenous knowledge seemed to be in line with the trend of the rising importance of the wisdom of traditional teachings providing a more holistic understanding of humanity's origins.

It is important to note that Hakim has received a formal education besides his traditional training and holds degrees from Cairo University in archaeology and Egyptology. He also did graduate work at Leydon University in the Netherlands, so his unique style of teaching combines an extensive education in the accepted paradigms of Egyptology and a deep understanding of the indigenous wisdom teachings of his native country. Many times in the field he has astounded me with his acumen as a trained archaeologist. Hakim often spoke to me of the indigenous tradition he adheres to (in the last few years of the 1990s), stating that he was chosen as a young boy by female elders of his tribe to be a future wisdom keeper. This connection to the matriarchal/matrilineal element fits very well into the traditions of ancient Egypt that I had previously researched. The indigenous tradition that Hakim represents is one of long-standing oral teaching and initiation that goes back thousands of years before the advent of writing. This tradition is similar to that of the African Griots, those who have maintained a detailed record of tribal history strictly by oral transmission for many generations.[4] Hakim also demonstrated a profound understanding of the meaning of the hieroglyphic symbols and the evolution of all modern written languages, information that played a vital role in the field work we did together, in the experiences we shared and in our development of new concepts.

Hakim had also presented me with the concept of an advanced civilization existing in ancient Africa well over 10,000 years ago, a civilization capable of working with stone such as limestone, granite, schist, diorite, basalt and alabaster with a sophistication and accuracy almost completely ignored by modern Egyptologists and scientists.

With my introduction to Christopher Dunn's theories in 1996 and the subsequent release of his book in 1998, the last piece fell into place for the creation of a whole new approach to the subject. Christopher Dunn has over 35 years of technical expertise in machining and engineering and has maintained that the precision and tolerances exhibited in the construction of the Great Pyramid are concrete examples of a people using advanced machining techniques, for the purposes of the structure functioning as a power plant. With Dunn's contributions I could now present a coherent theory, with ample physical evidence and examples, of the ancient wisdom espoused by the indigenous tradition of Abd'El Hakim. This tradition was obviously in conflict with the accepted paradigms of academic Egyptology, and I would have to discuss how these differences had arisen. It was also evident that I would have to present an adequate case for the failure of Egyptology to account for the anomalies Dunn and myself have observed and why and how their paradigms had evolved. In the next few chapters I will present this case and unveil the new ideas and concepts I propose to replace them.

CHAPTER THREE

EGYPTOLOGY AND ITS PARADIGMS

S AN ACADEMIC discipline taught in universities around the world, Egyptology is considered to be a recent phenomenon, only about 150 years old. Yet, its history can be traced back thousands of years. Egyptology has a rich legacy, which for our purposes I will touch upon only briefly. Much of the early writings about ancient Egypt came from the Greeks, who are considered to be the founders of the first great civilization of the Western world. Many of the Greek philosophers and writers traveled about and recorded their observations in some of the first travelogue accounts and histories. Mathematicians such as Thales and Pythagoras are said to have traveled to Egypt and acquired their knowledge and wisdom from Egyptian priests. But it was with the writings of two Greek historians, Herodotus and Manetho, that the history of Egyptology really began, and many of the accepted concepts in the field today are still based on their work.

Most people today accept that Egyptology is a rigorous discipline that fulfills all the prerequisites of a legitimate science. Since Egyptology deals with the study of ancient Egyptian antiquities, the ancient Egyptian language and cultural history, then as a discipline it falls under the larger umbrella of anthropology and archaeology. Anthropology is the study of Humankind, as compared to other animals, and the study of the distinctly human mechanism, culture. Archaeology uncovers and analyzes ancient artifacts and antiquities, the remnants of culture—so we see that Egyptology is the study of humans in ancient Egypt, their history, language and the artifacts of their material culture left to us to reveal and interpret. But since Egypt is part of Africa, not the Middle East, this study should also include the indigenous oral traditions of the peoples of modern and ancient Africa, which are almost completely lacking in the current academic pursuits of Egyptology.

Therefore, in order to present new paradigms based on indigenous wisdom teachings, stories and myths which appeal to a right brain, holistic understanding, and which greatly augment the left brain's interpretation of artifacts and structures such as pyramids and temples, it is necessary to understand how the current paradigms of Egyptology have evolved. Many serious students of this field venture forth without a sense of history, without an understanding of how their chosen discipline or field came to be set forth with its accepted paradigms. Without a historical framework and an understanding of the history of its paradigms, a science is empty and vacuous, and cannot, in my opinion, be fully comprehended and questioned.

Herodotus traveled to Egypt around 440 BC and wrote about his observations in the third volume of his *Histories*. There has been a constant debate, particularly in the last 100 years, as to the accuracy of his work, and even his intentions and motives. Peter Tompkins, in his book *Secrets of the Great Pyramid*, wrote, "in his *History*, which contains the first comprehensive account of Egypt to have survived intact, Herodotus deals with other [construction] aspects of the (Great) Pyramid, but not all his information can be taken at face value."[1]

So it was Herodotus who introduced the concept that the Great

Pyramid was built as a tomb for a king, the accepted theory in Egyptology today, and one which is strongly contradicted by the indigenous tradition. Herodotus' *Histories* did have a great impact on his country and people, causing many Greeks to became fascinated with the wonders of Egypt, including the great philosopher, Plato.

Plato attributed much wisdom and knowledge to the Egyptians in his *Dialogues*. Plato's student Aristotle in turn regaled his disciple Alexander of Macedonia with stories of the wonders of Egypt. Alexander was particularly interested in exploring Northern Africa when he began his conquests in the 4th century BC. When he annexed Egypt under Grecian influence, Alexander the Great left one of his generals, Ptolemy, to rule, and thus began what Egyptologists call the Ptolemaic period, 332-30 BC. A priest of the city called Sebennytus, named Manetho, compiled a history of Egypt around 270 BC. Only excerpts of his writings have survived into the modern era, but it was his paradigms of Egyptian history that also have formed a major basis for modern Egyptology.[2] Manetho divided the history of ancient Egypt by the reigns of kings in family lines, sons usually succeeding fathers, and he called these periods dynasties.

Many Greek and Roman travelers recorded histories of Egypt, such as Diodorus Siculus, Strabo and Pliny. With the Islamic invasion of Egypt in AD 640, most of the works of Greek and Roman historians were translated into Arabic, and with the later religious hostilities between Islam and Christianity, European interest in ancient Egypt was dormant for many centuries. Some of the works of Arab historians, such as Al Masoudi, Abd'El Latif, Ibn Batuta and Ibn Abd'Al Hokim, discuss stories and legends not known to the Greeks and Romans and that are almost completely ignored by modern Egyptologists.[3]

A few centuries after The Crusades, with the rise of interest in the sciences in Europe, travelers began to voyage back to Egypt. John Greaves, a British mathematician and astronomer interested in stories about the wonders of the Great Pyramid, went to Egypt in 1638. After exhaustive investigations on-site, he returned to England and published one of the first European works in Egyptology called *Pyramidographia*. Greaves' work influenced two other scientists, Tito Livio Burattini and Sir Isaac Newton, both of whom used Greaves' measurements in the hope of finding universals incorporated in the Great Pyramid. They hoped to use this data in order to be able to calculate geographical degrees for an accurate knowledge of the circumference of the Earth, mentioned by Greco-Roman authors as being known to the ancient Egyptians. In 1765, a British traveler named Nathaniel Davison also ventured to Egypt to explore the Great Pyramid. He discovered the first of five chambers above the so-called King's Chamber in the Great Pyramid.

Many Egyptologists, especially the French, consider modern Egyptology to have begun in 1798 with Napoleon's conquest of Egypt. To his credit, the ambitious Bonaparte brought with him 175 "savants," the term for the scientists of the time. Two of these savants, Dominique Vivant Denon and Edmé-François Jomard, made detailed sketches and measurements of the Great Pyramid and many of the then extant temples throughout Egypt. Denon produced two volumes of etchings which became tremendously popular in Europe and ended the paradigms from the Renaissance that great architecture and sculpture in stone had begun with the Greeks. The French produced 21 volumes of books under Napoleon's reign about their discoveries in Egypt. Perhaps the most important find by the French at this time was the famous Rosetta Stone, a slab of diorite found in 1799 by a Captain Bouchard near Rosetta, an area of the delta in northern Egypt. It contained inscriptions in three languages, hieroglyphic, Demotic and Greek. As no European had seen or understood Egyptian hieroglyphs, the fact that a Greek translation was present enabled scholars to finally decipher the ancient Egyptian symbols, based on that Greek understanding. A French scholar, Jean-François Champollion, labored for 20 years on the Greek, and in 1821 announced he had been able to translate the hieroglyphs.[4]

This feat truly began the science of Egyptology. Now that it was believed that the Egyptian pictographic writing could be translated into

French and English, inscriptions on temple walls and papyrus texts could be translated to create a framework for the history and culture of ancient Egypt, or so it would seem. However, the translation of Egyptian inscriptions and texts forming the major paradigms of Egyptology was accomplished by westerners, the French and British, from a western source, the Greek understanding of the ancient Egyptian hieroglyphic writing. Since the Greeks were interlopers, this means the current field of Egyptology is based on the perspective of people who were not part of the indigenous culture, who may have been, in fact, viewed with hostility by the indigenous wisdom keepers of that culture. This also could mean that the translations of the symbols given to the Greeks by Egyptian priests may have been incomplete in meaning; Abd'El Hakim has often suggested that this is exactly the case.

The next groups to enter the field of Egyptology, after the French and British, were the Italians and Germans. The Germans readily embraced archaeology and began visiting Egypt in the early nineteenth century. Karl Richard Lepsius led one of the first Prussian (German) expeditions to Egypt and paved the way for later German Egyptologists, such as Karl Brugsch and Ludwig Borchardt, and many others who contributed to the field in the late nineteenth and early twentieth century. The Italians had shown an interest in Egyptology even before the Germans, from the aforementioned Burattini of the seventeenth century, to later men such as Giovanni Belzoni and Giovanni Caviglia of the nineteenth century. Both Belzoni and Caviglia did early excavation work on the Giza Plateau and in the pyramids located there.

Other names that should be mentioned as Egyptology blossomed throughout Europe in the nineteenth century are those of the Frenchmen Auguste Mariette, whose work led to the founding of the Cairo Museum, and Gaston Maspero, author of many books in the field. The British were also well represented in Egyptology, with such names as Colonel Richard Howard-Vyse, who conducted many excavations at the Great Pyramid in 1837-1838, and Sir E. A. Wallis Budge, keeper of Egyptian Antiquities at the British Museum in the late nineteenth century. Budge was also the author of a major work of translation of a papyrus found in the tomb of a priest named Ani, which has come to be known as the *The Egyptian Book of the Dead.*

In my opinion, the greatest name of British Egyptology is that of the aforementioned Sir William Matthew Flinders Petrie. A surveyor and son of an engineer, he is credited as being the father of both modern archaeology and British Egyptology. Petrie conducted exhaustive surveys of the Great Pyramid in the 1880s and established the standards of excavation that all Egyptologists have had to live up to since. Petrie went on to produce many books on the subject, some of which are still considered classics in the field. Many later British Egyptologists, such as Margaret Murray, Alan Gardiner, Howard Carter, J. D. Pendlebury, Arthur Wiegall, Walter Emory and I. E. S. Edwards, were either students of or greatly influenced by the works of Sir Flinders Petrie.

The American entry into the field of Egyptology began in the late nineteenth century. James Henry Breasted of the University of Chicago is considered to be one of the first, if not the first, American Egyptologists and wrote many histories of ancient Egypt. George Reisner, representing Harvard University, began excavating in Egypt in the early twentieth century. Reisner, known for his extensive excavations on the Giza Plateau, made many discoveries around the Great Sphinx and Giza Pyramids. I should also mention John Wilson and Michael Hoffman as American Egyptologists who have added much to the field in the latter half of the twentieth century.

Presently Mark Lehner has done the most to follow up on Reisner's work and has led many excavations at Giza in the 1980s and 1990s. Lehner is considered the leading American exponent of the accepted paradigms of Egyptology and is the author of several books which I will discuss in greater detail later.

The contributions of Egyptian born Egyptologists should also be mentioned. Individuals such as Selim Hassan, Ahmed Fakhry, Zaki Saad and currently Zahi Hawass have represented their country's involvement with the study of ancient Egypt by conducting many important excavations and authoring several books. Dr. Hawass has recently made a great discovery of a cemetery at the Oasis of Bahariya in the Western Desert of Egypt, known as the "Valley of The Golden Mummies."

It is clear then from this brief history of Egyptology that the science has evolved from a strictly Western perspective. From the Greeks and Romans to the French, British, Italians, Germans and Americans, the field has been dominated by Eurocentric Western paradigms. Even the native Egyptian Egyptologists mentioned have been trained in the Western tradition of Egyptology, anthropology and archaeology.

There are, of course, many others who have written books and contributed to both the academic discipline of Egyptology and who have written alternative views on the subject. Some authors I have mentioned before: R. A. Schwaller de Lubicz, John Anthony West, Peter Tompkins and Murry Hope. Others whose work that I consider important can be found in the bibliography. Currently, I consider the work of Christopher Dunn, Abd'El Hakim Awyan and Karena Bryan to be the most important new contributions to the field in looking at existing evidence in a new light and offering an indigenous perspective not previously considered or respected by Egyptologists.

Currently, Egyptology enjoys its greatest influence and popularity. Egyptology departments exist in many universities in almost every leading country in the world. In 1999, there were groups digging in Egypt from universities in Japan, Poland, Sweden, England, Italy, Germany, France, the United States, Canada and of course Egypt itself. There is an unprecedented number of popular as well as academic books and articles appearing monthly on the subject and a constant stream of media presentations, television and radio shows dealing with some aspect of the subject. There is a plethora of websites on the Internet concerned with ancient Egypt, and any search engine will result in hundreds of references. But now there is also a growing tide of opinion outside the academic discipline of Egyptology that some major revisions in the accepted constructs of the field are at hand.

CHAPTER FOUR

TIME FOR A
PARADIGM SHIFT

"THE TRANSITION FROM a paradigm in crisis to a new one from which a new tradition of normal science can emerge is far from a cumulative process, one achieved by an articulation or extension of the old paradigm. Rather it is a reconstruction of the field from new fundamentals, a reconstruction that changes some of the field's most elementary, theoretical generalizations as well as many of its paradigm methods and applications . . . a useful elementary prototype for what occurs in a full-scale paradigm shift."[1]

These thoughts, written by Professor Thomas S. Kuhn in the 1950s, challenged the way we think science works. He introduced the concept of "paradigm shift" and expanded on the definition of what paradigms are. Kuhn stated in 1969, "The term 'paradigm' is used in two different senses. On the one hand, it stands for the entire constellation of beliefs, values, techniques and so on shared by the members of a given community. On the other, it denotes one sort of element in that constellation, the concrete puzzle-solutions which, employed as models or examples, can replace explicit rules as a basis for the solution of the remaining puzzles of normal science."[2]

It is in this second sense that Kuhn developed the controversial concept that science is normally a subjective and irrational enterprise. He skillfully argued that once paradigms are fixed, most scientists are not even open to contrary ideas. Kuhn also argued that science does not change gradually, as when accumulated data calls forth a paradigm shift (a term as shown in the preceding quote Kuhn introduced), but it takes a revolutionary process, the radical introduction of brand new ways of seeing already gathered data and information to manifest a full-scale change in scientific thinking.

Professor Kuhn's work itself serves as a perfect example of his own thesis. He cited historical cases of the changes in many areas of science which occurred as the result of radical shifts in thinking, not by gradual changes in theories created by mounting accumulations of data. Kuhn established the concept of paradigm shifts being sudden and dramatic and science changing by revolution, not evolution. This concept, being itself revolutionary, was soundly criticized by many scientists in the 1960s, in essence proving Kuhn's point that most scientists were subjectively locked into their own paradigms and were not open-minded, objective viewers of new, radical ideas.[3]

These radical shifts most often occur outside the academic field they influence, not from those professors firmly entrenched in their disciplines. The most classic example is that of Albert Einstein, who developed his Special Theory of Relativity while working as a patent clerk in Switzerland and later became a professor of physics.[4] Increasingly, by necessity the demand for paradigm shifts within a particular science must come from outside the field as the adherents of that science have become so absorbed into their mutually accepted paradigms that they literally cannot "see the forest for the trees" and cannot even decipher the origins of their paradigms. This is, I believe, the state of the field of academic Egyptology today! Thomas Kuhn argued vehemently for scientists to be aware and cognizant of history, the history of their discipline and the history of its paradigms. The major reason I included a chapter on the history of Egyptology is for that elucidation; many Egyptologists are aware of broad histories of excavations and finds but not of how their paradigms have been derived. The deeply embedded paradigm of science and history beginning with Greco-Roman culture precludes by its very nature the possible existence of an indigenous Egyptian culture that could have a sense of it own history and prehistory.

It is not enough, then, just to know that the foundations of the paradigms of Egyptology were based on the observations of Greek authors, but we must understand the paradigms those Greek authors themselves operated on. For example, Herodotus, often called the "Father of History," in his writings described his impressions of what he was supposedly told by Egyptian priests. But Herodotus recorded his impressions from his own world view, a Greek perspective, and that perspective was a patriarchal one. Patriarchal cultures are mainly concerned with male descent patterns, from father to son, and with kings who passed their power and property in inheritances to their male heirs. But, as I and many other authors have argued, ancient Egypt was predominantly throughout its history (and prehistory) a matriarchal culture, and descent was matrilineal, power and property being inherited from mother to daughter. Herodotus, with patriarchal paradigm filters, never observed this phenomenon, and therefore assumed Egypt to be as Greece, controlled by male kingship patterns.

On this basis, it is not clear whether Herodotus did not understand the histories told to him by the priests, or whether the priests deliberately told untruths because of his cultural misconceptions. Herodotus may have deliberately presented false information because he was under oath to the indigenous wisdom keepers not to reveal the truth to the uninitiated. The indigenous tradition I have uncovered seems to hold to the former, that Herodotus was considered part of an invading patriarchal culture, and as an interloper, was not told the truth of Egyptian history and culture. Manetho, a priest serving under Grecian Ptolemaic patriarchal rulership of Egypt, wrote "histories" of Egypt based upon "dynasties" of male kingship, as if this was the genuine paradigm of Egyptian social structure and history. Again, we do not know if Manetho, perhaps being a Greek rather than an indigenous Egyptian wisdom keeper, was writing what he knew a Greek audience would be able to understand or relate to, or if he was sincerely ignorant of true Egyptian matrilineal social history. He, also, may have taken a vow to the indigenous wisdom keepers to obfuscate the real history. The reasons the true history may have been kept from the Greeks by the Egyptian priests was because the Egyptians regarded the Greeks as "barbarians," with no real sense of their own history and prehistory, and in Egypt it was only the initiated who learned the ancient wisdom teachings.

It is from the writings of Herodotus and Manetho that the basic paradigms of ancient Egyptian history and social structure were formed by Egyptologists. But it is evident how shaky these paradigms are from the statements of Egyptologists themselves. As Mark Lehner points out, "In the writings of the Green historian Herodotus we do indeed find a mixture of fact and folktale about the Pyramids . . . it was Herodotus who established the erroneous and now virtually ineradicable association between pyramid building and slave labour."[5] It is ironic that Lehner finds fault with Herodotus about how the Great Pyramid was built but has no problem accepting Herodotus' story that the function of the Great Pyramid was as a tomb for a king! Lehner also states that Manetho was an Egyptian priest (it is not definitive whether he was indigenous or Greek) and had written his history "possibly to correct the chronology of Herodotus . . . . Our framework for ancient Egyptian history is still based on Manethos' king list."[6] Lehner then states that Manetho credits Khufu, written in the Greek form Suphis, with building the Great Pyramid. So in actuality, Manetho, writing in Greek for a Greek audience, was not differing at all from Herodotus as both were inculcated in a Greek patriarchal paradigm of a civilization based primarily on kingship and pyramids as tombs for these kings, two basic paradigms that Egyptologists such as Mark Lehner readily accept.

Yet, there have not been any inscriptions, reliefs, texts or even an original burial found in any major Egyptian pyramid that indicates that pyramids were tombs for kings. Again Mark Lehner states, "Burial rituals enacted at the pyramid ensured the transfer of kingship from the dead pharaoh to the living one . . . Much of our information for Egyptian funerals comes from scenes in tombs of high officials, since the king's funeral is never shown in any of the pictorial fragments recovered from pyramid temples."[7] The assumption remains that pyramids were tombs for kings, even though Lehner clearly states there has never been any evidence found, pictorial or scriptural, of a funeral taking place in a pyramid. Lehner also states that funerals were certainly depicted on tomb walls of nobles. If pyramids were tombs also, why are there no depictions of a king's funeral in so-called burial chambers? There are the Pyramid Texts (which should be called "Funerary Texts"), but no translations of these texts ever mentions an actual burial of a king in a pyramid. I will return to a discussion of these Pyramid Texts in another context, but it should be clearly understood that in the major Egyptian Pyramids, those found at Dahshur, Sakkara, Abusir and Giza, no inscription, text, or relief in any so-called burial chamber has ever been found indicating that any king or anyone else was originally intended to be buried there.

Not only do we find the paradigm of pyramids as tombs in need of revision, but the accepted theories of how pyramids were built are also sorely lacking in substantive evidence. The tool kits found by Egyptologists and claimed by them to have been used to build the pyramids, namely copper chisels and drills and stone pounders, have been challenged by many authors as being woefully inadequate to accomplish the task. The stone material used by the ancients, basalt, granite, diorite and alabaster, cannot be readily cut and shaped by even the best of copper tools. The strongest challenge to this inadequate paradigm has been put forth by master craftsman and engineer Christopher Dunn in his excellent book *The Giza Power Plant*. Dunn clearly establishes in his book that the evidence found by Sir William Flinders Petrie and himself indicates lathes, tubular drills and perhaps ultrasonic machining, or some other sort of sophisticated techniques, must have been used to cut and shape granite and basalt. Dunn also points to the multiple contoured angles and precision and tolerances of 2/10,000 of an inch in shaped Egyptian stone of granite, basalt and alabaster as further examples of advanced machining technology used by the ancient craftspeople and engineers. The angles are too precise and the tolerances too fine to be explained in any other way (*see* Figure 8).

Figure 8.
Giza Plateau. Author standing next to a worked (machined?) piece of granite. 1999. Photo by Christopher Dunn.

Not only are the basic accepted paradigms of Egyptology concerning descent patterns (matrilineal not patrilineal), importance of kingship, reasons for and methods of construction of pyramids and other structures inadequate, but their basic understanding of and the translations of written and inscribed material may be in need of revision. As mentioned, it was the discovery of the Rosetta Stone in 1799 and its decipherment by Jean-François Champollion in 1821 that has enabled Egyptologists to translate the hieroglyphs of the ancient Egyptians wherever found. It has always been assumed that the Greeks who dominated Egypt after Alexander the Great in 330 BC were themselves able to completely and correctly translate the symbols. What if there were hidden meanings to the symbols which were not transmitted to the Greek interlopers by the indigenous Egyptian priests? What if the Greeks were told only mundane superficial meanings, and those were the meanings used by Champollion as he phonetically arrived at his translations from the Greek section compared to the hieroglyphic section of the Rosetta Stone? This, of course, is exactly the scenario proposed by R. A. Schwaller de Lubicz in his writings and his creation of the school of thought that has been called Symbolist Egyptology.[8]

Schwaller proposed there were different levels of understanding used by Egyptian priest-scribes in writing their sacred texts, different levels of understanding according to the levels of wisdom achieved by the observer. The symbols contained levels from mundane and superficial to profound and metaphysical, with different degrees of initiation required to understand the depth of the symbols and the wisdom contained therein. Therefore, it is quite possible that all the translations presented by those followers of Champollion's paradigms, Egyptologists such as Wilkinson, Budge, Breasted, Gardiner, Edwards, Lehner and Hawass, are of the mundane level only and are therefore superficial and not completely accurate. Further examples of this will be presented in the next chapter, but here I would offer the works of R. A. and Isha Schwaller de Lubicz, Lucie Lamy, Bika Reed and Normandie Ellis as translations of texts that may be more in alignment with what the ancients intended. In particular, the book *Rebel in the Soul* by Bika Reed features a fresh translation of a known Egyptian papyrus with a greater metaphysical understanding than what was presented previously by Egyptologists.

Even more so, I present the translations of Abd'El Hakim Awyan and the indigenous wisdom keepers of Egypt as the basis for the fuller and richer meanings of the glyphs. It may be that only those indigenous wisdom keepers like Hakim, representing an oral transmission of and initiation into a profound understanding of the symbols, are able to fully translate those symbols for all the rest of us.

As Thomas Kuhn noted in the perceptions of members of the physical sciences of the 1950s, and in the staunchly stubborn attacks against his thesis by academicians in the social sciences of the 1960s, paradigms do not metamorphose or perambulate into change by gradual acceptance; they disappear through radical revision by dramatic, revolutionary actions. Alternative researchers, operating outside of the paradigms of academia, are currently promoting this revolution by presenting their ideas to the public through books, articles, conference presentations, media interviews and on websites on the Internet worldwide. The last ten years have seen a virtual cyber information explosion in all areas of thought, and the present number of websites devoted to some aspect of ancient Egypt is overwhelming. Many individuals are calling for new ways to explain aspects of Egyptology from a holistic perspective on many Internet forums and chat groups. It is time, according to higher cyclical cosmic patterns, to fully present the indigenous wisdom of Egypt to the whole world.

CHAPTER FIVE

KHEMITOLOGY — NEW PARADIGMS

MY MEETING AND subsequent tutelage with Abd'El Hakim from 1992 to the present now forms the framework of a viable, comprehensive system for the creation of not only new paradigms but a whole new discipline. This system has been introduced by Hakim and Karena Bryan in their book *Egypt and the Awakening*. I will give a summary of some of these teachings in order to create the framework that will enable us to erect the structure for the material to be presented.

The information Hakim has given to me even challenges the name of the discipline and the ancient country itself. Egypt is the name of the present country located in Northern Africa. The word "Egypt" is based on the Greek word, *Aegyptos*, but few have bothered to investigate its origins. "Aegyptos" is a contraction of the term *Hi-Gi-Ptos*, which was a Greek transliteration of the ancient term *Hit-Ka-Ptah*. *Hit* (or *Het*) means place and *Ka* has been translated by Egyptologists in many ways, but I use the definition "the physical projection of the soul"—not the body which was *Khat* or *Khet*, but the personality which attaches itself to the body in metaphysical terms. Ptah was the title of one of the so-called "Creator Gods," a *Neter*, the meaning of which I will discuss in more detail in this chapter.

So the term *Het-Ka-Ptah* in essence means "The Place of the Projection of the God Ptah," or "The Place Where the Projection of Ptah Manifested." This term can be found as an inscription on a stele (stone slab with writings or symbols upon it) near the modern Egyptian village of Mit Rahaina, situated on the ruins of the ancient capitol city the Greeks named Memphis, known to the ancients as *Men-Nefer* (the Generation of Harmony). Therefore the term *Het-Ka-Ptah* only referred to one site, the city that became the first capital of the so-called dynastic period of ancient Egypt, not the whole country or civilization (*see* Figure 9). The ancients themselves referred to their "country" as *KMT*, which has been written many different ways, *Kemit, Kemet, Khemet, Khem, Al Khem*—and in the form we choose, Khemit. It literally means "The

Figure 9. Memphis. Abd'El Hakim pointing to glyphs *Het-Ka-Ptah*, the origin of the word Egypt. Stele of Apries. 1998. Photo by author.

Black Land" and referred to the rich, dark, alluvial, fertile soil deposited by the Nile River, which made possible the agricultural basis of the civilization (*see* Figure 10). The indigenous tradition tells us the civilization was Khemit, the people and language were both called Khemitian. There

Figure 10.
KMT, Khemit-The Black Land.

was no "dynastic" differentiation in the matriarchal indigenous understanding, only prehistoric and historic Khemit.

Therefore, the initial indigenous teaching is to discard the name Egypt, and the title Egyptology, completely. The new discipline is *Khemitology*, based on an oral tradition long established before Greek written records, long before the advent of any known written language, a tradition existing for many tens of thousands of years. The Arabs, who entered the land after AD 200, were certainly aware of the ancient indigenous tradition, as illustrated by their use of the term *Al Khem* for the present country of Egypt. This is the source of the modern word "alchemy." The Greek word "chemistry" no doubt was derived from Khemit also, and both alchemy and chemistry were considered to be "Egyptian arts." Indeed, all modern arts and sciences may have originated in ancient Khemit. The concept of alchemy as being the obsession of individuals in the Middle Ages in European history attempting to transform lead into gold is just about as superficial an understanding as the Greeks apparently had of Khemit itself. Those who study alchemy seriously know that the concept of turning lead into gold is a metaphor for a complex system of transformation of the self, a path to enlightenment.

Since the research efforts of Margaret Murray, Barbara Lesko, Merlin Stone and myself have already challenged the Greek-inspired paradigm of a patriarchal ancient Khemit with a social structure emphasizing male kingship and descent patterns, we can now discard that paradigm and replace it with the indigenous teaching of a matriarchal Khemit with predominantly matrilineal descent. One of the first things that attracted me to Hakim's teachings when I first met him in 1992 was his insistence on the primacy of matrilineal descent in ancient Khemit and the supreme role women played in the civilization, a paradigm I had been espousing since 1977. Now we have the indigenous Khemitian teachings to concretize this paradigm of Khemitology.

We all have heard and used the word "pharaoh" synonymously with the word "king," and usually with a male connotation. Even most academic Egyptologists have not traced the origins of the word "pharaoh," which is a Greek derivation of the Khemitian term *Per-Aa* which means "High House" and does not refer to a male king, but to the female, the Khemitian head of the household (*see* Figure 11). Why did so many men consort with their full and half sisters, even their daughters and mothers, in ancient Khemit (so-called dynastic Egypt)? It is primarily because power, status and property descended through the female line, from

Figure 11.
Temple of Hathor at Dendara. Abd'El Hakim pointing to cartouche with the term *Per-Aa,* High
House, which referred to the female head of the
royal family, not the male king. Origin of the word
pharaoh. 1998. Photo by author.

mother to daughter, and in order for men to gain a position of status and
rulership, they had to align themselves with the heiress to that position,
oftentimes their own sister—not for any predilection to incest but to conform to accepted patterns of social structure.

Egyptologists teach us that the model of kingship was based on the
mythology of Isis, Osiris and Horus. They don't often mention that the
symbol of Isis is the throne, that she was the power of rulership and by
consorting with her brother Osiris, she enabled him to have the position

of "Good King" (*see* Figure 12). When their son Horus avenges his father's murder by the "evil" uncle/brother Set, Horus—the Khemitian word *Hor* or *Heru* is the source of the Greek word "hero"—is the risen Osiris, the ruling "Good King." While the Greeks placed the emphasis on Horus as the ruler, the male king, the Khemitians emphasized Horus'

Figure 12.
Temple of Osiris at Abydos. Isis (left) and her brother-consort, Osiris. The throne on Isis' head was her symbol of royal power. 1999. Photo by author.

consort, *Hat-hor*, meaning the "Place/House of Hor," as being the *Per-Aa*, the "High House." As Isis gave the power of the throne to Osiris, it is by virtue of Hathor that Horus is given kingship. This is the ancient indigenous tradition, one that the Greeks reversed in importance. Hakim also teaches that the symbol on Isis's head is a great chair, as the woman known as *Hemeti*, being the head of the household, is to be treated with respect and given comfort, to sit with her feet resting on a footstool.

The realization of the role of women in ancient Khemit is the first major challenge to the modern paradigms of Egyptology. The great Egyptologist Margaret Murray (the first woman to get a Ph.D. in the field) was largely ignored when she wrote in the late 1940s, "In any sociological study of ancient Egypt the status of the women must be clearly understood . . . they [women] enjoyed a peculiar position from the fact that all landed property descended in the female line from mother to daughter."[1]

Even 50 years after these words were published, the emphasis in Egyptology is still male kingship and "dynasties" of fathers and sons. In her autobiography, *My First Hundred Years*, Dr. Murray often expressed her loneliness as the only woman in the field in the early part of the twentieth century and how she had to suppress many of her ideas for fear of ridicule from her male colleagues.[2]

Many researchers, such as W. Marsham Adams, Manly P. Hall, Paul Brunton, H. Spencer Lewis and Christopher Dunn (as well as myself) have challenged the paradigm of "pyramid-as-tomb." Now I will present the indigenous teachings to create a new explanation of the purpose of the pyramids. As I introduced *Per-Aa* to show the Khemitian origin of the Greek word "Pharaoh" (in Hebrew "Per-O"), I now present three more Khemitian terms, *Per-Ka*, *Per-Ba*, and *Per-Neter*. *Per-Ka* means the "House of the Ka" (physical projection) and was the place where the dead body (*Khat*) was placed, or the tomb. In most ancient societies, the body was usually placed in the ground or in a cave away from predators (particularly the jackal in Africa). The ancient Khemitians dug a hole and eventually put a stone slab over the grave, which the Arabs call "mastaba" (bench). This was the *Per-Ka*, and Egyptologists teach that the pyramid was a logical extension of the mastaba, as in the famous Step Pyramid of Sakkara. The Step Pyramid is a built-up mastaba, as one layer was added on top of another until the structure we see today was created. But Hakim has always been adamant, according to his tradition, that the Step Pyramid of Sakkara was a late innovation and is a glorified *Per-Ka*, not a true pyramid. The *Per-Ka* or tomb was usually something that was to be dug into the Earth, either in bedrock, mountains or under the sand, and did not "evolve" into a true pyramid.

The next term, *Per-Ba*, translates as the "House of the Soul or Spirit" and became the Temple, the place of prayer, meditation, chanting sacred sounds and ritual—practices to uplift and raise consciousness. The *Per-Ba* appears very early in Khemitian prehistory, and the oldest such structures are still under the sands of Egypt. Hakim gives a profound explanation going back to the mists of prehistory for the origin of temples. The beginning of each temple was an area, usually with a source of crystal and running water. A few stones would be placed on an altar, the stones crystalline in nature, and the altar would be of igneous rock (granite, basalt, or alabaster). This area was the "first" sacred site, the running water and crystal combining to create an active energy field. This is where people went to "get high," to experience altered states of consciousness, to commune with "God." This initial area would be the "Holy of Holies," originally available to all the people. Later in late prehistorical or early historical times, walls, courtyards, pylons and gates were added and the *Per-Ba*, the temple, was born.

When I first went to Egypt in 1992 and visited the Temple of Luxor, a typical dynastic Khemitian Per-Ba, I was told by a guide, in confidence, that a recent (1992) repair project to some columns in the courtyard complex of the temple had uncovered the tops of other columns underneath the present ones, thus revealing an older Khemitian Per-Ba under the present temple. The find was quickly "covered up" and has never been disclosed publicly. Of course, stories like this one abound in all phases of archaeology, but Hakim confirmed this particular story in 1998 when we were at the Temple of Luxor. This is, I believe, a perfect example of a sacred site where an ancient Per-Ba would be located and a later people built a newer temple on top of the older one. Perhaps because of its value as a tourist attraction (or for whatever reason), no reported excavation to uncover an older Per-Ba under the current Temple of Luxor has taken place.

The fourth term I cover here is the most revolutionary. The Khemitian term *Per-Neter* is the basis for the Greek concept of pyramid (*see* Figure 13). The word "pyramid" is derived from the Greek words *Pyramis* and *Pyramidos*. The meaning of *Pyramis* is obscure and may refer

Figure 13.
Abusir. The glyph *Per-Neter*, the Khemitian term for pyramid on a slab of granite. 1997. Photo by author.

47

to the shape of a pyramid. *Pyramidos* has been translated as "Fire in the Middle" and does not seem to pertain to or connote a place of burial. The word *Neter*, sometimes rendered as Netjer by Egyptologists, has sparked much debate in the last 40 years or so. First translated by early Egyptologists after Champollion as "God" or "Goddess," this meaning has since been challenged. R. A. Schwaller de Lubicz was one of the first to question this translation in the early 1950s, choosing rather to define *Neter* as "principle" and/or "attribute," as a divine aspect of the whole, not in the sense we use the word Deity.[3] The Greeks derived their word Nature from *Neter*, therefore equating the Divine with the natural (as the Khemitians taught them). The ancient Khemitians knew every principle or attribute of Nature was also divine, "of God"—all interconnected and interrelated to the whole, the source. This is the holistic understanding exhibited by all indigenous teachings, and now proclaimed by quantum physicists, that of the interconnectedness of all things.

In the indigenous Khemitian tradition as taught by Abd'El Hakim, *Neter* is also translated as "sense," as in our five senses, an aspect of consciousness. Hakim teaches that we have 360 senses, or Neters, within our innate being, and 355 are dormant in most people at the current time. Many times in the field Hakim has "turned on" some of the Neters, the dormant senses, for me and I have never felt more alive and aware, senses aflame like an animal, providing an experiential knowing of his teaching. In fact, the particular role that Hakim has been trained for by his masters and elders is to "turn the key" at the sites, to open the energy and allow people to experience the Neters personally.

Therefore, I translate *Per-Neter* as being the "House of Nature" and "House of Energy," and thus being fundamentally different than a *Per-Ka* (the house of burial) or *Per-Ba* (the house of prayer/meditation/ritual) (*see* Figure 14). Working in accordance with the laws of God and Nature, the original intent of the *Per-Neter* was to generate, transform, utilize and transmit energy. In this respect I state, categorically and emphatically, that in its original intent, no one was ever to be buried in a Per-Neter. In fact, there is no proof that any body or part of a body has ever been found in a true Per-Neter anywhere in Khemit/Egypt that is an original burial. All bodies or parts of bodies that have been associated with some Per-Neters or found therein have been identified as an intrusive burial done many thousands of years after the active function of the Per-Neter had ceased. In other words, long after the Per-Neter no longer functioned in its original use, priests may have had individuals buried near or in the ancient Per-Neters to identify with the greatness of their ancestors. By this

Figure 14.
Graphic depicting the symbols for *Per-Neter* (pyramid) and *Per-Ba* (temple). Image created by Robert M. Vawter, 1998.

new definition of the function of a pyramid, any mummy or parts of a mummy found therein would be an intrusive burial. Even Mark Lehner, one of the staunchest defenders of the pyramid-as-tomb paradigm, has stated that no original burials have ever been found in any Egyptian pyramids.

Egyptologists are currently adopting a series of hieroglyphs they translate as "MR Pyramid" to be the Khemitian term for pyramid. Mark Lehner states, "The word for pyramid in ancient Egyptian is *Mer*. There seems to be no cosmic significance in the term itself. I. E. S. Edwards, the great pyramid authority, attempted to find a meaning from *m*, 'instrument' or 'place', plus *ar*, 'ascension', as 'place of ascension'. Although he himself doubted this derivation, the pyramid was indeed a place or instrument of ascension for the king after death."[4] Even admitting his "great pyramid authority," the late keeper of Egyptian Antiquities of the British Museum, I. E. S. Edwards, doubted that *MR* could relate to a "place of ascension," Lehner staunchly adheres to his tomb-for-king paradigm. Our indigenous authority, Abd'El Hakim, translates *MR* as *beloved*, as in Meriamen (Beloved of Amen, the Hidden One) or Meritaten (Beloved of Aten, The Wiser), and *MR* has nothing to do with Per-Neter, the Khemitian term for pyramid.

As Per-Neter meant "House of Energy," Christopher Dunn in his book *The Giza Power Plant* has radically challenged the accepted view by proposing the Great Pyramid functioned as a power plant, a theory that properly aligns with the indigenous concept of Per-Neter. Dunn has suggested the Great Pyramid acts first as a seismic tap, resonating in harmony with the Earth's basic vibrational energy, and resonates with the igneous rocks present such as granite, diorite, schist and basalt, along with the highly organic sedimentary rock, limestone, to generate a harmonic acoustical amplification of that basic energy.[5] The pyramid would then act as a delivery system, a power plant for the practical application of this energy. Many different authors are now proposing their own theories as to how the Great Pyramid would act as an energy device, including theoretical physicists from the former Soviet Union.[6] Of course, I also recognize other functions of the Great Pyramid and will discuss these also.

The radical proposal espoused by Christopher Dunn lays the groundwork for an even larger paradigm shift not only for Egyptology but for larger areas of human evolutionary theory. Dunn does not concern himself with when and who built the Great Pyramid, but with the how and why. The how and why he proposes are indeed revolutionary in themselves, and I will add the who and when in this book. The who should be clear by now, the ancient Khemitians, not aliens nor Atlanteans, as I have broached this area before in relating the alleged finds of Dr. J. O. Kinnaman. But before I develop the full picture of when the ancient Khemitians accomplished this great feat and present alternative views of their possible connection with the myth of Atlantis and extraterrestrial contacts, I must finish laying the groundwork for the new paradigms. For now I present the indigenous tradition that the major Per-Neters of Khemit (Giza, etc.) were constructed well over 10,000 years ago, along with the ancient Per-Bas, many of which still lay hidden under the desert sands. Not only did the ancient Khemitians possess advanced machining and sophisticated engineering skills as proposed by Christopher Dunn, but they also possessed a knowledge of science, mathematics, metaphysics, natural laws, and esoteric wisdom thousands of years before civilization, according to accepted paradigms, is supposed to have existed.

Other authors have tread this ground before and have led the way for this great paradigm shift. David Hatcher Childress, Gunnar Thompson, Graham Hancock, John Anthony West, Michael Cremo and others have all presented arguments for advanced human civilization existing thousands of years prior to academic theory. D. S. Allan, J. B. Delair and Paul LaViolette have challenged accepted theories of geology and anthropology by stating great cataclysmic events about 11,500 years ago could have virtually eliminated traces of prior advanced civilizations. Only a few remaining great stone structures, such as the Sphinx and Pyramids in Egypt, Stonehenge in England, Tiahuanaco in Bolivia, Baalbeck in Lebanon and others scattered around the world, are remnants of previous human advancement prior to 10,000 years ago.

I join with these authors and propose, according to the indigenous teachings, that the ancient civilization of Khemit may have stretched back over 65,000 years ago. There may also have been prior stages of civilization that went even further back, into ages past that few researchers would venture to speculate about. The proposed idea is that great cataclysmic events, such as one about 11,500 years ago, may have eliminated almost all traces of ancient civilizations, which are only kept in our collective memories through the myths and stories of indigenous wisdom keepers. John Milton, Michael Cremo, Richard Thompson and Lloyd Pye have severely challenged the accepted Darwinian paradigm of linear human evolution, and I agree with Cremo and Thompson, who present the Vedic belief that human development has been in cycles rather than in a straight line. This is also in accordance with the indigenous Khemitian tradition, that all things move in cycles, including human development, and nothing is ever totally lost.

As presented in their book *Egypt and the Awakening*, Abd'El Hakim Awyan and Karena Bryan delineate the Khemitian tradition of cycles as being simple, yet profound. Schwaller de Lubicz had stated the Khemitians used the known to invoke the unknown. Observed cycles and events in the natural world can imply unseen, spiritual and metaphysical cycles—in essence, as above, so below. Hakim teaches the same basic understanding that daily cycles reflect great epochal and cosmic cycles. The daily movement of the sun in the sky is a great Khemitian teaching that also reflects stages in human development.

These movements are called the five stages of the sun. To the Khemitians the sky was a feminine principle, depicted by the body of the Neter ("Goddess") *Nut* who gave birth to the sun (her son) at dawn and swallowed him again at night. A great diurnal cycle of life was created that was basic to Khemitian daily existence. Dawn, the birth and emergence of the sun after the night of darkness, was called *Kheper* (The Driller), named after the scarab beetle. The second stage when the sun was at high noon was *Ra* (The Stubborn), the most commonly known name from the literature. The third stage as the sun moved across the afternoon sky was

Oon (The Wise). The stage of the sun when it was at its fullest expression was *Aten* (The Wiser), representing late afternoon. The last stage is *Amen* (The Hidden) as the sun is swallowed by Nut and disappears into night once again.

These stages were also used to represent stages of consciousness in the developing human experience. Kheper, the Driller, was the Dawn of Consciousness (the innocence of childhood), the first step on the path to enlightenment. Ra, the Stubborn, was the ego stage of consciousness (also referred to as adolescence), too stubborn to let go of rational thought after a little knowledge had been accrued. Oon, the Wise, was a mature consciousness when wisdom had been obtained. Aten (Itn), the Wiser, was when consciousness was in full flower and a constant state of enlightenment reached. Lastly, Amen (Imn), the Hidden, was when all light disappeared and greed, fear and darkness pervaded.

These stages also reflect actual Khemitian designations of stages in human history. The current cycle of Khemitian civilization is estimated to have started with a Kheper phase, a dawn over 65,000 years ago.[7] We are now considered to be nearing the end of an Amen stage of the entire cycle, begun perhaps 4-6,000 years ago and coinciding with our current patriarchal era of massive warfare, rampant uncontrolled growth and technology, in which almost all human systems are out of balance and devoid of true spiritual content, immersed in ignorance and darkness. This Amen stage corresponds with the rise of so-called dynastic Egypt which was only a shadow of the Khemit of prehistoric times.

We are now being told by all indigenous wisdom keepers that a great change in human consciousness is indeed imminent. The major reason for the disclosure of the indigenous Khemitian teachings now is the belief that we are finally at the end of the Amen stage of darkness and soon to start a new cycle of Kheper, a new Dawn of Consciousness. In this respect, the indigenous Khemitian master Abd'El Hakim has joined many other indigenous teachers (Vedic, Tibetan, Mayan, Aztec, Hopi and other Native American) who are claiming we are coming to an end of many coinciding cycles mentioned by the different traditions at this point in time.

Another major area to be considered is who these ancient Khemitians were. A popular movement among many African-American scholars in the last 30 years has been to claim a strictly Black African heritage for Khemit, as modern Egypt is certainly located in northeastern Africa. This movement has been called "The Nile Valley School" and has had many adherents among African-American academicians. Much of this belief is based on the writings of Senegalese scholar Cheikh Anta Diop, who wrote books on the subject in the 1950s and '60s. Diop argued that ancient Khemit was entirely Black African and that prehistoric Africa had many great advanced civilizations. Because of racist tendencies among white European scholars, these prior African civilizations have been almost totally ignored. Diop also argued that Khemit did not refer to the black soil of the Nile deposition, but the Black skin color of its people.

A coinciding movement amongst many scholars in the last 30 years or so, labeled "Afrocentrism," has promoted the paradigm that almost all of the trappings of European civilization began thousands of years earlier in Africa. I have discussed these theories with Hakim often in the last few years. While he is very proud of his Black African blood (on his mother's side), Abd'El Hakim's view differs strongly. Hakim is adamant that Khemit meant the Black Land and did not refer to the skin color or any race of the Khemitian people. Yet Hakim is a profound Afrocentrist because he believes ancient Khemitian and African cultures were highly advanced well over 10,000 years ago.

In explaining the origins of the Khemitian people, Hakim has maintained there is a key number that appears throughout his indigenous mythology and teachings. It is the number 42, and this is because ancient Khemit was composed originally of 42 tribes. These 42 original tribes were composed of all known races and peoples; Northern Africa is considered to be one of the original gathering places of all races from throughout Africa and the world that created great civilizations many thousands of years before the Greeks or anyone else. Examples of the 42 tribes can be seen carved on the walls of the great Per-Bas, obviously showing all races evident in Khemit. I, personally, have observed examples of all peoples and races shown in the art of Khemit and in the current groups of people living in Egypt today. To claim that ancient Khemit was a Black African civilization could be considered essentially reverse racism and reflects a bias that does not lead to a complete understanding of the greatness of the ancient Khemitians. To see the faces of the people of Egypt today is to see a melange of all the humanity that has ever been on this planet, both as the original humans who evolved in Africa, and all the people who have settled in Egypt in the last 10,000 years, and the 42 tribes were indeed all people, known in Khemitian as *The Sesh*.

The concept of *Sesh* cannot be overemphasized for a complete understanding of the Khemitian indigenous wisdom. The Sesh were the composite of the 42 tribes and meant all people, regardless of race or gender. Tribal identity remained important even in so-called "dynastic" times in terms of what were called *Nomes*, believed to be geographical areas. In reality these were tribal lands, yet racial differences were not reasons for separate classifications to the Khemitians, as all were considered The Sesh. It is my distinct opinion that the concept of race and the practice of racism is a modern by-product of the age of Amen, patriarchal darkness, and did not exist over 6,000 years ago, and certainly was not known to the ancient Khemitians.

The Khemitian language spoken by the Sesh may have been one of the original languages spoken by humans on this planet. The Arab tongue spoken today in Egypt is actually 80 percent Khemitian and 20 percent Hebrew, the Arabs having entered Egypt after 200 AD. Hebrew itself, considered by philologists (those that study language) to have been derived from ancient Indo-European tongues such as Sanskrit, may itself have been fully derived from ancient Khemitian. This is not an original hypothesis; a French scholar at the time of Napoleon, Fabre d'Olivet, wrote *The Hebraic Tongue Restored* in 1815 in which he argued that the Hebrew language of the Old Testament was derived solely from ancient Egyptian. Ancient Egyptian was, of course, the Khemitian language, and still lives in modern

Hebrew and Arabic. The Old Testament story of the Tower of Babel, where once all peoples (The Sesh) spoke the same language, may be a metaphor for the 42 tribes all speaking the same Khemitian tongue. Once they dispersed to different lands and continents, the different languages we speak today evolved.

The accepted academic paradigms state writing began around six thousand years ago in ancient Sumer (modern Iraq) and then somehow moved into Khemit. The indigenous Khemitian tradition states that writing may have begun two to three thousand years earlier and actually started in Khemit. Ancient Sumer may have been a part of Khemit. The word *Sufi*, which means literally in Arabic "man of wool," is normally defined as relating to a group of Islamic mystics still very active today.[8] Sufi is derived from the Khemitian word *Suf*. The indigenous tradition teaches that *Suf* means "the written language of Khemit" and is the original, proper word for the written script the Greeks labeled *Hieroglyphica* (sacred symbols). The term "Sufi" may refer to those adepts who originated the symbols and passed their esoteric meanings down in secret from master to disciple for many thousands of years. They later became assimilated into Islam, but have maintained a system of a secret, oral tradition that may be the basis of Sufism today. The "wool" of the Sufi is the fiber of the cocoon of the butterfly chrysalis, a "birth" fiber, the Suf language being the birth of all written symbolic scripts.

The proper use of language and the origins of modern tongues from Khemitian is one of the fundamental indigenous teachings of Abd'El Hakim. Even the word *Hebrew* itself does not escape this paradigm of Khemitology. Traditionally defined from the appearance of Abram in Genesis of the Old Testament (before he became Abraham), it supposedly meant "to cross over"; Abram is referred to as "The Hebrew," as he crossed over the River Jordan to Canaan to settle.[9] Egyptologists believe the word *Hebrew* is derived from the Khemitian words *Apiru* or *Habiru* which meant "foreigners" or "strangers" and would imply the Hebrews, as Semites, were of different lineage than the Khemitians, in support of the Old Testament presentation. But the indigenous Khemitian tradition does not support the contention that the Hebrews were strangers and foreigners to the Khemitians; instead they may have been part of the original 42 tribes. Many times what comes down to modern languages as an "H" sound in more ancient tongues was "Kh," the guttural sound "ch" heard in Arabic and Hebrew. Hakim teaches that the word *Hebrew* is derived from the Khemitian term *Kheperu*, the plural form of Kheper, the scarab beetle which represented the rebirth of the sun as dawn, the beginning of consciousness. This could indicate the Hebrews were originally an indigenous Khemitian people who were in existence many thousands of years before any historical figure who could be known as Abram or Abraham, and were present at the very Kheper stage of Khemitian prehistory, at "The Dawn of Consciousness."

This may seem quite speculative, but until now many of the paradigms of ancient history were formulated to conform to Western Judeo-Christian beliefs as presented in the Old Testament. The Old Testament itself was created to formulate a history and a mythology for a displaced people, the Jews, after their displacement, the Diaspora, by the Assyrians and the Babylonians. I will undertake a complete discourse on this subject in a second book, but many authors, especially Sir Laurance Gardner and Ahmed Osman, have recently argued we should use other sources of knowledge and attempt to reconcile the Old Testament to these sources instead of the other way around as has been the case for many years.

The indigenous Khemitian teachings presented here represent an oral tradition purportedly going back many thousands of years before the Greeks entered Khemit, and many thousands of years before the so-called "dynastic" period which began ca. 3100 BC. These teachings provide a framework from which to develop the new paradigms of Khemitology and from which to interpret archaeological and geological data already presented by previous researchers. The indigenous tradition speaks of an ancient civilization and people, existing well before the proposed theory of a major global cataclysmic event occurring over 10,000 years ago.

In Part Two, I will present the data and observations gathered in the field to support these new paradigms and to provide a cultural context for an ancient Khemitian civilization. I will amplify the work of Christopher Dunn in ascribing to the ancient Khemitians advanced capabilities in engineering, machining, anti-gravitics and abilities to produce and transmit energy in accordance with sophisticated knowledge of all sciences and natural laws.

PART TWO:

THE LAND OF OSIRIS

DEFINITION AND OVERVIEW

I N THE NBC Television Documentary entitled "Mysteries of The Sphinx" first aired in November 1993, author and independent Egyptologist John Anthony West and Boston University geologist Robert M. Schoch presented detailed evidence to support the theory that the body and enclosure of the Great Sphinx of Giza, Egypt, was eroded by water, specifically rainfall. Since there has not been significant rainfall in that area of the world in over 5-10,000 years, it was then speculated upon by both men that the Sphinx must have been carved out of the living rock much earlier than its accepted date of 2500 BC or approximately 4500 years ago. To account for the massive water-induced erosion, West has further suggested the Sphinx may be over 10,000 years old.

Mark Lehner, in questioning West and Schoch's work and the theory that the Sphinx could represent an older "Egyptian" civilization, put forth a significant criticism. Lehner stated that if indeed there was a civilization prior to dynastic Egypt that created the Sphinx, where is the other evidence of such a civilization? Stating there was "a problem of a lack of a cultural context" for an earlier Sphinx, Lehner's classic comment was "show me a potsherd!"[1]

As a supporter of the work of West and Schoch, I took Lehner's comments as a challenge for major field investigation at the archaeological sites of Egypt to see if indeed there was any evidence to provide answers for Lehner's queries. The first major breakthrough in this regard was accomplished in November 1996 by Bob Vawter. In the years since my initial visit to Egypt in 1992, Bob and I had spent many hours discussing the preliminary teachings of Abd'El Hakim that I had brought back with me. Although I had kept track of Hakim through other sources, such as his tours with Barbara Hand Clow, there had not been any direct follow-up contact between us. With funding for our project hard to come by, Bob and I planned return trips to Egypt in 1993-1995, but they did not materialize. Finally, using his own resources, Bob journeyed to Egypt by himself in November 1996 and reconnected with Hakim personally. This began the flow of information of the indigenous tradition of Khemit that has continued ever since and provides the framework presented here.

When Bob returned from his field work with Hakim, he shared with me the indigenous Khemitian teachings I had not experienced before. Bob kept mentioning discussions of an ancient part of Khemit that Hakim referred to as Bu Wizzer. Hakim continually emphasized the pivotal importance of the concept of Bu Wizzer in realizing the great antiquity of ancient Khemit. As mentioned previously, further discussions with Hakim took place in Alameda, California, in August 1997, which led to the Kinnaman Foundation sponsored expedition to Egypt in September of 1997. Bob and I were able to spend ample time in the field with Hakim and develop the framework and find the evidence presented in this and succeeding chapters. The indigenous tradition tells us that the area known as Bu Wizzer or The Land Of Osiris was one of the earliest settled areas of Khemit, and this is where we have searched for archaeological and geological evidences of the ancient Khemitian civilization.

I already defined Bu Wizzer as The Land of Osiris which referred to a geographical area composed of the sites of Dahshur, Sakkara, Abusir and Abu Ghrob, Zawiyet el Aryan, Giza and Abu Roash (*see* Figure 15).

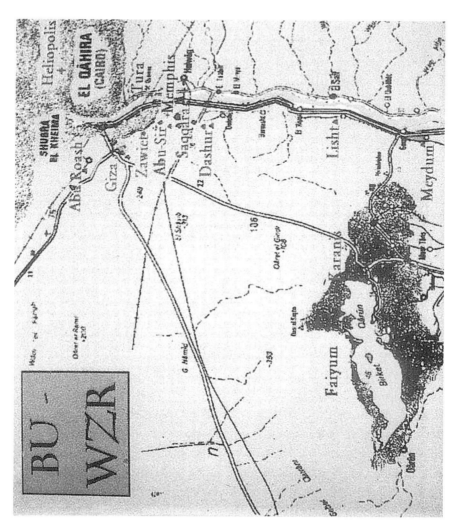

Figure 15.
Map showing *Bu Wizzer* sites from north to south. Image created by Robert M. Vawter. 1998.

Bu is the ancient Khemitian term for land, and *Wizzer* (also written *WZR*) is the correct Khemitian title for the "God" or Neter the Greeks named Osiris, also called Osar or Ausar. Who Osiris was has been the subject of much debate by various authors. The classic Egyptologist E. A. Wallis Budge considered him a mythological concept, while author Zecharia Sitchin has indicated in his books that he may have considered Osiris to have been an extraterrestrial. Certainly, he was a much venerated figure in all of Khemitian history. According to the indigenous tradition, Wizzer was considered to be one of Khemit's early leaders, whether mythological or an actual man, a prototype for later kings, who introduced the Sesh to agriculture, architecture in stonework, engineering, law, spirituality, science, ethics and all the trappings of modern civilization, in essence, bringing the people out of their early primitive state.

Most people who study Egyptology become very familiar with the mythology of Osiris-Isis-Horus as a basis for dynastic Khemitian civilization. I have discussed this mythology as the basis for kingship theories in the Greek translations that formed the patriarchal paradigm taught by Egyptologists. The importance for us here is not to concentrate on Wizzer as a patriarchal model of kingship, but as an ancient ruler who brought the early civilization into focus.

Bu Wizzer is a defined geographical area which existed within Khemit. As mentioned, it includes the sites from south to north as the Nile River flows: Dahshur, Sakkara, Abusir and Abu Ghurob, Zawiyet el Awyan, Giza and Abu Roash. Although Egyptologists have stated these sites came into existence during so-called dynastic time periods, particularly the "Old Kingdom" ca. 2700-2100 BC, we maintain that all of these sites that make up Bu Wizzer are originally from a prehistorical Khemitian civilization that was in existence over 10,000 years ago. Part Two will present our investigations at the Bu Wizzer sites and speculation on how they may have been connected and worked together.

One of the pivotal teachings of the indigenous Khemitian tradition as presented by Abd'El Hakim is that the present Nile River was not the river used by the prehistoric Khemitians. I first became familiar with a concept of an older Nile River in the book *Egypt Before the Pharaohs* by American Egyptologist Michael Hoffman in the early 1990s. It was in this book that Hoffman presented the theory of an older, larger river once in existence in what is today the Western Desert of Egypt. This ancient river has been called the *Ur Nil* or the Protonile by several geologists, and its very existence is also a matter of debate amongst scientists.[2] In 1997, Hakim promised to show me evidence that the four main Oases present today in the Western Desert, known as Bahariya, Farafra, Dakhla and Kharga, are the remains of this once huge, ancient Nile River. In the field work I did with Hakim in 1997 and 1998, he kept on insisting that I "follow the water" in order to develop the hypothesis of an ancient *Ur Nil*. This would be the evidence, he maintained, to establish the paradigm of ancient Khemit being over 10,000 years old, drawing its water sources from the west, where today only desert and the Oases exist.

The great global cataclysm, mentioned by many authors as having occurred approximately 11,500 years ago, radically altered geophysical and climatological conditions around the world. Rainfall, which once was so abundant in Northern Africa and which had created lush vegetation, lakes and mighty rivers, virtually ceased, resulting in dramatic shrinkages of water sources and the development of desert conditions. Water, crucial to all life, played a particularly important role in the ancient Khemitian civilization.

The following chapters will present the results of four trips to Egypt to work in the field with Abd'El Hakim and search for the evidence of Bu Wizzer and the ancient Ur Nil River. With our new paradigms of Khemitology as a framework, I was able to observe and record much in the field and to realize the extensive knowledge the ancient Khemitians had about the physical properties and potential uses of water, that miracle liquid so many of us take for granted. The Khemitians had several terms for water, but one, *Asgat*, will be the term I will focus on to present a primary understanding of the original conceptions used to build many of the structures at the Bu Wizzer sites. Per-Neters in particular were built for many purposes, some very practical reasons, not as tombs for, or even at the whims of, kings—but by a group of master engineers-scientists-priests who had long ago acquired a profound understanding of natural law and the knowledge of how to overcome the supposed limits of physics.

CHAPTER SEVEN

DAHSHUR

I START WITH THE site that is the southernmost border of Bu Wizzer, today called Dahshur, in the south because the Nile in all its permutations has always appeared to flow from south to north. The maps of the ancient Khemitians would have been reversed from those of ours today as they would have had the south at the top and the north at the bottom, following the flow of the river.

Dahshur is located approximately fifteen miles to the south of the famous area of the Giza Plateau. There are several structures still evident at the site, including two well known Per-Neters called today the Bent and Red (North) pyramids, respectively. There are several other structures located a mile or so east of these two Per-Neters, also called pyramids by Egyptologists but which are no doubt Per-Kas (tombs), built many thousands of years later. The current Nile River runs about six to eight miles to the east of the Dahshur Pyramids, and the area today is virtually all desert. Egyptologists contend the Nile was closer to the site when it was active, but the evidence we found pointed to the contrary.

An interesting paradox exists at Dahshur with respect to the structures found there. Egyptologists have decided that the site dates originally to the Old Kingdom period of dynastic Egypt due to some inscriptions found which contain cartouches. A *cartouche*, which literally means in French "a bag of holding" or grocery bag, is used by Egyptologists to mean a knot of papyrus scrolls in which they believed is inscribed a King's name. The indigenous tradition states that it was only titles that were contained in a cartouche, either titles of the king, tribal designations, or even the titles of the sites or structures themselves. Using the Greek derived paradigm of cartouches containing a king's name, the term found inscribed on ruins near the pyramids, *Sneferu*, is believed (by Egyptologists) to be a king who ruled about 2550 BC, specifically the first king of the 4th Dynasty of the Old Kingdom according to their chronology. Egyptologists have translated the term *Sneferu* as "He of Beauty."[1] But Hakim translates *Sneferu* as "Double Harmony," not an individual's name, but a term that may refer to the site itself with its two ancient Per-Neters, or to the structures found at the site.

All the literature of Egyptology assumes an individual king had the main structures at Dahshur built as his tomb. The other structures that are found to the east of the main pyramids at Dahshur are believed to have been constructed just a few hundred years later and are dated to the Middle Kingdom period of orthodox Egyptology (*see* Figure 16). But therein lies the paradox; only believed to be separated by a few hundred years, the supposed pyramids of a king "named" Sneferu of the Old Kingdom are vastly different from the structures of the Middle Kingdom period. They are also located in, apparently, the wrong place. The Middle Kingdom structures, constructed mainly of mudbrick, are almost all in ruins today (*see* Figure 17). Located east of the older structures, they are closer to the Nile as she is today. The older Per-Neters, constructed of limestone, basalt and granite, are further out into the desert. If they were indeed constructed during the 4th Dynasty as Egyptologists claim, why were they built far away from the river, in a desolate area? The Middle Kingdom structures at Dahshur were built to the east of the older Per-

Neters, closer to the Nile as it would have been at that time period, approximately 1900-1700 BC.

Figure 16.
Dahshur. Middle Kingdom pyramid in ruins. 1997. Photo by author.

Figure 17.
Dahshur. Close-up of Middle Kingdom pyramid, built mostly of mudbrick and virtually in ruins. 1997. Photo by author.

I contend the Middle Kingdom structures, built of inferior materials (mostly mudbrick with some small limestone blocks) and with inferior engineering skills, were not built by the same people as the stone masonry pyramids. I also postulate that those Middle Kingdom structures were not Per-Neters, but Per-Kas, and were only used for tombs, whether actual burials or symbolic ones. The Red and Bent Pyramids are true Per-Neters, never originally intended for anyone's burial and built many thousands of years before dynastic time periods (*see* Figures 18 and 19).

With the framework of the indigenous Khemitian teachings as our working paradigms, our observations on site provided a far different understanding of the area around the two Per-Neters of Dahshur. We took soil samples at several different places around both pyramids and found evidence of silt, pottery, bone chips and limestone, basalt and granite fragments. The silt is indicative of water sources under the desert sand, as well as the possibility of water present on the surface in ancient times. The potsherds found demonstrated an active site, either of occupation or pilgrimage, and the many varied styles indicated many thousands of years of both occupation and pilgrimage. Bone chips indicated sacrifices or sacrificial meals, also indicative of a sacred site. It was the limestone, basalt and granite fragments that provided the greatest speculation on our parts. Abd'El Hakim showed us evidences of many structures once present around the two pyramids at Dahshur. We saw remains that suggested limestone walls once stood to form channels for man-made canals to bring water to the site, with the basalt and granite fragments being the remains of docks for an artificial lake once near the Bent Pyramid. All these structures would have to have been built long before the current desert conditions, which would mean many thousands of years before the so-called 4th Dynasty period ascribed to the pyramids by Egyptologists.

Moreover, the direction of the flow of the water to these remnants of limestone walls, remains of docks and an ancient lake were from the west, not the east where the Nile is today. This would indicate the water flowing to the ancient site of Dahshur came from the Ur Nil, which may have

Figure 18.
Dahshur. Red (north)
Pyramid. 1997.
Photo by
author.

Figure 19.
Dahshur. The Bent
Pyramid. 1997.
Photo by
author.

dried up due to severe climatic changes over 10,000 years ago. I believe this evidence to be suggestive data to support the indigenous tradition of a much older Khemitian civilization that built the two Per-Neters, called the Red and Bent Pyramids. The evidence of other structures and water channels on the site negate the view that these pyramids were built for a egomaniacal king as his possible tombs in a desolate desert area.

Figure 20.
Dashur, north of Bent Pyramid, facing east.
Remains of limestone structures can be seen. It is possible these are the remains of docks for an ancient artifical lake over 10,000 years ago. 1999.
Photo by author.

Our observations inside the Red Pyramid confirmed our notion of it as a Per-Neter, a practical device for generation, transformation, utilization and transmission of energy. Robert Vawter, trained as a musician and acoustical engineer as well as a field archaeologist, was able to do preliminary sound experiments and recordings in September 1997 that indicated the Red Pyramid creates harmonic resonance at a different frequency than other pyramids. I took some sound recordings of the three of us (Bob, Hakim and myself) chanting vowel sounds in all the different chambers of the Red Pyramid. Later, Bob was able to process the recordings through his sound equipment and to synthesize some of the frequencies. He found overtones and resonance effects that recorded at different frequencies than those measured previously by other researchers in

70

the Great Pyramid. This evidence enabled us to speculate that the Per-Neters may have been "tuned" to different frequencies to resonate harmonically with each other (*see* Figure 21). Hakim also had us do some meditations in the different chambers of the Red Pyramid to connect with the energies still present. I was able to "feel" the pyramid still humming, still vibrating at a specific frequency set by the ancient Khemitians many thousands of years ago. We were unable, in 1997, to get inside the Bent Pyramid to perform sound tests and observations and hope to be able to do so at a later date.

Figure 21.
Dahshur. Upper walls of inner chamber in the Red Pyramid. Recessed walls are similar to Grand Gallery in the Great Pyramid, possibly used for harmonic acoustical resonance effects. 1997. Photo by author.

The orthodox Egyptology view of the so-called Bent Pyramid is that it was built before the Red Pyramid and represented a "mistake" in construction. The bottom section of the pyramid rises at a sloped angle of just under 55 degrees, but about halfway up "bends" to a sharper angle of 43 degrees (*see* Figure 22). The "mistake," according to the orthodox view, is that there was too much internal stress on the infrastructure of the core masonry with the 55 degree angle, so the builders had to adjust to a 43 degree angle to complete the structure.[2] Hakim rejected this explanation by stating there were "no mistakes" in the ancient Khemitian's large scale constructions, and the Bent Pyramid was intentionally designed and built the way it is. This is not to say the ancient Khemitians were infallible, but that people operating in full consciousness would not be likely to make such a mistake in building a Per-Neter. The Bent Pyramid is a true Per-Neter and was purposely built the way it was for principles of energy production through acoustical harmonic resonance by virtue of its unique shape. The Red Pyramid, at a 43 degree angle, may vibrate in a specific harmonic with the Bent Pyramid, and that also may be the reason for the term "Double Harmony" (Sneferu) at the site, not a specific king's name.

Figure 22.
Dahshur. The Bent Pyramid, northeast corner showing two angles of construction. 1999. Photo by author.

In May of 1999, I had detailed discussions with Christopher Dunn while we were in Egypt together, and we discussed these possible reasons for the term Double Harmony. He suggested that the Bent Pyramid, with its two angles of construction could produce multiple frequencies of sound, and this may be, in itself, the reason for the term Double Harmony.

We specifically examined in 1997, at Hakim's direction, the area from the southeast corner of the Red (North) Pyramid to the northeast corner of the Bent Pyramid. This is where we took our soil samples and also found water marks on elevated sand dunes where we believe the ancient river was channeled to the area (*see* Figure 23). These watermarks and silt deposits have been explained by Egyptologists as being from Nile flooding during the Old Kingdom period, but the apparent direction of the water coming from the west refutes this explanation. If indeed, the direction of the water flow can be established to have been from west to east,

Figure 23.
Dahshur. The Red Pyramid, facing north. Elevated sand dunes show evidence of silt deposits. Limestone, granite and basalt fragments in foreground are evidence of more structures originally present at this site. 1997. Photo by author.

then it could not have been from the current Nile River (*see* Figure 24).

Much more investigative work needs to be accomplished at Dahshur to completely determine what the site was about. In complete disagreement with accepted paradigms, I do not see that the Red and Bent Pyramids were built by the same civilization that built the Middle Kingdom mudbrick structures in ruins further east. The working hypothesis is that the two Per-Neters were built over 10,000 years ago as energy devices at the southern border of Bu Wizzer.

Figure 24.
Dahshur. The Bent Pyramid, facing west. The terrain seemed to slope from west to east, supporting the contention of a water flow in ancient times from the west. 1997. Photo by author.

SAKKARA

THE FAMOUS SITE of Sakkara (also written Saqqara) is located a few miles north of Dahshur and about eight to ten miles south of Giza. Currently it is believed that as many as eleven pyramids, in various states of ruin, may be found at Sakkara. However, it is doubtful which ones may have been true Per-Neters. It is obvious Sakkara was used as a necropolis in many different time periods in dynastic Khemitian history, as many tombs and burials are to be found there. The name Sakkara itself was from the Neter *Sokar*, considered to be a protector of the West, the land of the dead.

Many hundreds of tombs found in the Sakkara region, covering thousands of years of the dynastic period alone, confirm the site's status as a sacred burial area. But Egyptologists do not ask the question why this particular area was chosen by the dynastic Khemitians as a final resting place for so long a time period. Being west of the current Nile River (about eight miles), the site does fit the tradition of the west being the place where the spirit travels after death of the body. The indigenous tradition tells us that there was no word in the ancient Khemitian language for death; when the body ceased to function, it was said the spirit was "westing" or "going to the west." But was Sakkara chosen as a sacred place to the dynastic Khemitians because it had once been a vital ceremonial energy center for the ancient Khemitians many of thousands of years before?

Sakkara contains many structures of significance from many different time periods. At the site is the famous Step Pyramid and surrounding complex, one of the most visited areas for tourists in the last 150 years or so (*see* Figure 25). The orthodox Egyptology theory is that Sakkara was first used as a necropolis in the earliest stages of dynastic Khemitian history, beginning with the so-called 1st Dynasty ca. 3000 BC and continuing until the end of the Old Kingdom period ca. 2100 BC. There is even evidence that later periods, the Middle Kingdom era of ca.1800 BC and the 18th Dynasty of the New Kingdom period ca.1300 BC, also used the area for tombs and burials. British Egyptologist Walter Emory did much excavation work at Sakkara from 1936-1956, uncovering many of the

Figure 25.
Sakkara. Step Pyramid and surrounding structures. 1992. Photo by author.

early dynastic tombs and structures and finding several interesting arti-facts, including a cache of stone pottery, plates and bowls. Later French Egyptologist Jean-Phillipe Lauer did much of the excavation of the Step Pyramid complex. It was primarily the archaeological work of Emory and Lauer that has formed the accepted paradigms of Sakkara being mainly a necropolis site originating in Old Kingdom dynastic Khemit.

Most Egyptologists believe simple pit-tombs covered by stone slabs (mastabas) evolved into pyramids for tombs. This is exemplified by the Step Pyramid, believed to have been constructed under the direction of the physician priest Imhotep for a king named Djoser (Zoser) in the 3rd Dynasty of the Old Kingdom period ca. 2650 BC. It is further believed the whole surrounding complex around the Step Pyramid was built at the same time as part of a ceremonial center enclosing the King's burial in the Step Pyramid.[1] Very little scriptural or documenting evidence exists to support all of these beliefs, but they have become foundation paradigms of Egyptology. The pyramid is seen as evolving from a sequence of events: from pit-tombs to mastabas, then the addition of more stones going higher up, culminating in the Step Pyramid as the first attempt to construct a massive tomb for a king. The sequence of construction of the Step Pyramid seems to support this view as at least three to four different stages of construction seem to show the evolution of the structure from simple mastaba to a six stepped pyramid about 200 feet high. But accord-ing to the indigenous Khemitian tradition, the Step Pyramid was origi-nally a Per-Ka, a tomb that was stepped and enlarged to resemble a Per-Neter. It is, therefore, younger, not older, than the true Per-Neters dis-cussed in this section. The Step Pyramid never really functioned as a Per-Neter. The indigenous tradition states the Step Pyramid is at least 6,000 years old, at least 1300 years older than its accepted Old Kingdom date, but that the surrounding enclosure was not built at the same time and is over 12,000 years old. The enclosure is obviously built of different mate-rials than the pyramid, and it is only assumed that Imhotep had the whole complex constructed at the same time. There are neither records nor any direct proof that the complex was built all at the same time—there could easily be thousands of years of differences in various sections of the Sakkara complex.

The walls of the enclosure are made of a distinctly yellowish limestone that does appear to be very old. Hakim points out that the style of the enclosure resembles Mesopotamian architecture and may have ancient Sumerian influence (*see* Figure 26). But if it was constructed over 12,000 years ago, it would represent an ancient Sumer in existence over 6,000 years before academia recognizes the beginnings of the civilization of Sumer. Hakim has often stated that there was a prehistoric Sumer that was part of Khemit, and it was not until historical times (4000 BC) that the Sumer recognized by academia developed its own unique culture.

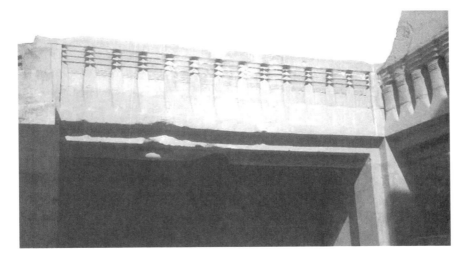

Figure 26.
Sakkara. Part of enclosure walls with Djed pillars. Limestone of enclosure appears much older than Step Pyramid. Evidence of Mesopotamian-style architecture, according to Abd'El Hakim. 1997. Photo by author.

I have had many opportunities to be in the field at Sakkara with Abd'El Hakim, and our observations there have been some of the most profound. While Egyptologists have become concretized in their Old Kingdom paradigms, we have been able to literally look beneath the surface (*see* Figures 27-31). What we have observed is an elaborate tunnel system existing everywhere at the Sakkara sites. Many of these tunnels have been exposed by previous excavations with little or no commentary by Egyptologists. Mark Lehner refers to underground chambers or passages under the Step Pyramid as part of Djoser's funerary cult, but makes no mention of the myriad of tunnels all over the Sakkara area.[2]

Our observations seemed to confirm the indigenous tradition of the tunnels being constructed by the ancient Khemitians as water channels. Water was channeled to the site for energy, the water acting in harmonic acoustical resonance with the igneous rocks of the Per-Neters and related structures. It appeared to us that the water was channeled from the west, the direction of the ancient Ur Nil, not the current river about eight to ten miles to the east of Sakkara. The downward sloping of the ground was from west to east, and the tunnels seemed to be coming from the west also. The tunnels and channels we observed were in different layers of bedrock under the surface, cut in rectangular, smooth-sided, serpentine passages going, apparently, for miles under and through the limestone bedrock. These passages all seemed man-made, not natural formations. The major reason Egyptologists do not comment on these tunnels is because it damages their "Old Kingdom Paradigm" of copper tool kits and stone pounders as the technology used—these tunnels appear to have been cut with advanced machining techniques using sophisticated concepts of engineering.

Hakim told me a story of an event that occurred when he was about 17 years old and investigating the tunnels at Sakkara. He wandered into one tunnel and followed it for many hours. He later emerged out of a tunnel on the Giza Plateau some eight to ten miles away! Of course, one can argue this is just a "story" and cannot be verified, but there is no doubt from our on-site investigations that Sakkara is literally honeycombed

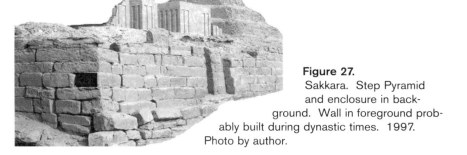

Figure 27.
Sakkara. Step Pyramid
and enclosure in back-
ground. Wall in foreground probably built during dynastic times. 1997.
Photo by author.

Figure 28.
Sakkara. Further to the
left (south), exposed tunnels
going through limestone bedrock.
1997. Photo by author.

Figure 29.
Sakkara. Still further left (south),
more tunnels evident deeper in
bedrock. 1997. Photo by author.

Figure 30.
Sakkara. Closer shot
of layers of tunnels
going through lime-
stone bedrock. 1997.
Photo by author.

Figure 31.
Sakkara. Close-up
of shaft going
straight down into
bedrock. Abd'El
Hakim estimates
shaft goes down
over 300 meters
(1,000 feet). Notice
relatively smooth,
almost right angle
walls. 1997. Photo
by author.

with tunnels, some going down hundreds of feet into the bedrock. Interestingly enough, in 1997 when Hakim attempted to show us this very same tunnel he had ventured into as a young man, we found it covered over by a concrete slab (*see* Figure 32). The Supreme Council of Antiquities in Egypt, which governs all the archaeological sites, would probably justify this concrete slab as protection for the tourists, but other tunnel entrances are evident at Sakkara with just fencing or nothing around them for protection (*see* Figure 33). Why was that one covered over? Could it be because someone else could follow that path and prove the tunnels connect, at least all the way to Giza? If indeed the ancient Khemitians drilled these miles of tunnels to draw water from the ancient Ur Nil in the west, then Sakkara must have been an active living site, not a necropolis, over 10,000 years ago as the indigenous tradition asserts.

Figure 32.
Sakkara. Abd'El Hakim standing on concrete slab covering tunnel that may lead to Giza, some 8-10 miles to the north. 1997. Photo by author.

Figure 33.
Sakkara. Hole leading to underground tunnel with no protection around it. 1997. Photo by author.

It would also be apparent that these tunnels were drilled and cut long before the above ground structures were built as drilling tunnels under pyramids and temples after they were built could compromise their structural integrity. I felt, therefore, the underground passages represent decidedly older archaeological layers. What was truly amazing to me was that so many of these tunnels were previously exposed, that we did not have to undergo any major excavations to find them. I am sure if we were granted the permits and had the proper funding to undertake major excavation work, we could uncover many more miles of these tunnels and be able to trace them further out into the Western Desert—at least, be able to test this hypothesis more rigorously, one way or the other.

Sakkara is one of Hakim's favorite areas, and he has literally spent many hundreds of hours in investigation there. Hakim always leads people to certain areas southeast of the Step Pyramid where he believes an elaborate complex for healing once existed. The indigenous tradition maintains that one of the major functions of the entire Sakkara area in ancient Khemitian times was for healing by the use of sound. All that remains of the ancient structures are walls constructed of limestone that once held 28 niches, 14 on each side. Some of these niches still exist, and Hakim encourages people to place their heads into the niches to experience the energy still present (*see* Figure 34). In ancient Khemitian times, a patient would place their heads in the niches, and a healer-priest(ess) would stand on a nearby platform and intone a series of sounds. By the use of the sound vibrations, the healer would be able to see a holographic image in their mind's eye of the patient's complete body, a sort of MRI where blood and lymph flow, organs, tissues and energy-flows through the nervous system could all be seen. Blockages of all aspects would become known to the healer, and as soon as these images were seen, a conscious connection would be made from healer to patient, and the healing process would automatically begin. Many current alternative healing modalities utilize these same principles. Hakim has always maintained that Sakkara was an ancient healing site utilizing sound as the medium, and only much later, in early dynastic times, did the area become a vast

Figure 34.
Sakkara. One of the still extant healing niches
south of the Step Pyramid. 1992. Photo by
author.

necropolis.

It was at Sakkara that Hakim first demonstrated his ability to teach from the right-brain and "turn the key" to open the energy of the sites for me. In November 1992, when I first visited Sakkara with Nicki Scully's group, Hakim lectured to us about the healing niches and the ancient use of sound for healing. He suggested to our group that we do a meditation circle on the platform where the ancient healers would stand to do their sound invocations. As it was starting to get dark, the guardians and antiquities police urged us to return to our tour bus as all the sites are supposed to close at sundown. Hakim encouraged us to continue and chased everyone away from disturbing us. As we began to meditate, Hakim joined our circle, sitting down next to me and taking my hand. I felt a tremendous upsurge of energy, and for a few brief moments, all time and space seemed to stand still. I then felt our entire circle spin and create a vortex of energy, spiraling upward. When I came out of meditation, Hakim was smiling at me, and I knew he had created the effect. This, of course, was a totally subjective experience, but to me it was the first indication of Hakim's role as a *Keeper of The Keys* and his ability to unlock the energies at the sites.

Then in 1997, Hakim was able to provide some material evidence for the left-brain scientific experience. In August of 1997, I had a meeting with Hakim in Alameda, California, to prepare for our expedition to the Bu Wizzer sites in September of that year. Hakim promised he would show me the ruins of a "Mayan" temple in Egypt. On site in September 1997, he took me to some structures about a mile south of the Step Pyramid complex. There were the remains of a small temple supposedly built in the 18th Dynasty of the New Kingdom period (ca. 1300 BC), according to accepted orthodox chronology. The temple has been attributed to an individual named *Maya*, but Hakim is adamant that this was a title, not a name, that there was no individual named Maya (*see* Figure 35). Interestingly, maya is one of the terms used today in Egypt for water. Hakim suggests "Maya" was a title of an individual who may have come from Pre-Columbian Central America to Khemit—perhaps "Maya" meant "from across the water" to the Khemitians. But this seemed like a stretch, pure speculation, without any empirical data. Observing the ruins in 1997, I commented to Hakim there was really nothing to base this theory on—the site looked decidedly dynastic Khemitian. One of the site guardians, a Keeper who did not speak any English, noticed my perplexed state and motioned me to follow him to a small chapel enclosure.

We pulled away some wooden boards blocking the stone doors and threw open the enclosure. On the ceiling were some unusual geometric glyphs that did not appear to me to be typically Khemitian in style (*see*

Figure 36, color insert). I later sent a photograph of these glyphs to Mayan Daykeeper Hunbatz Men in November 1997. I had gotten his mailing address from Aluna Joy Yaxk'in, a student of Hunbatz Men whom I had met earlier. Hunbatz graciously answered my letter and stated that it was his belief that those glyphs were ancient Mayan as he recognized the style, patterns and color sequences as belonging to the tradition of his ancestors (see Appendix A). He even claimed he could recognize two of the glyphs. Of course, this flies in the face of accepted paradigms of academic Mayan archaeology as the chapel, even if recognized as 18th Dynasty Khemitian, would make those glyphs at least 3,300

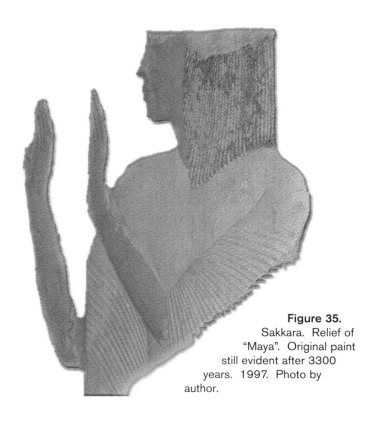

Figure 35.
Sakkara. Relief of "Maya". Original paint still evident after 3300 years. 1997. Photo by author.

years old, perhaps 1,000 years before the Maya were supposed to have come into existence as a civilization!

In February of 1998, I also showed a photograph of the ceiling glyphs to another Mayan Elder, a well known healer (curandera) and priestess, named Flordemayo. While she could not state definitely the glyphs were ancient Mayan, her first impressions on seeing the photo was that the ceiling was from Mexico or Central America. She was later amazed to find out the site was in Sakkara, Egypt. I gave Flordemayo some reprints of the photograph of the ceiling, which she said she wanted to show to her teacher. Later I saw Flordemayo at a conference in Sedona, Arizona in April of 1999. She excitedly told me she had shown the images to her teacher, Mayan Elder Don Alejandro Cirilo Oxlaj Peres, one of the recognized leaders and wisdom keepers of the indigenous tradition of the Quiche Maya in Guatemala, and he had confirmed that the glyphs were, indeed, ancient Mayan. Don Alejandro had related an Indigenous Mayan teaching that the ancient ancestors of the Maya had come "from the stars" to four areas of the world. One of those areas was ancient Khemit where they were called the *Naga Maya*. When I presented this information to Hakim in May of 1999 in Egypt, he was very pleased at the indigenous confirmation of the find. In October of 1999, while on tour with Hakim in the south of Egypt, he stated to me that the word *Naga* was from the ancient Khemitian word *Ng* or *Nag*, which meant tribe. So the term *Naga Maya* in ancient Khemitian could have meant "the tribe that came from across the water."

Also found at Sakkara are remnants of other pyramids built during the 5th and 6th Dynasty periods of Khemitian history. These pyramids are mostly in ruins and would appear to have been Per-Kas, not Per-Neters. The most famous one is called the Pyramid of *Unas*, supposedly the last king of the 5th Dynasty (ca. 2350 BC). Hakim states the title, not name, should be *Wenis*, not *Unas* (read as W.N.S.). The construction style of this pyramid shows the use of small limestone blocks and no granite or basalt, greatly inferior to the Per-Neters at Dahshur or Giza. On the walls of the structure are the famous so called "Pyramid Texts," the subject of much speculation in recent books. The standard orthodox view has held that the texts are a series of protective spells or prayers to enable the dead king's soul to emerge and rise to higher realms unscathed. Others such as Alexander Badawy, Jane Sellers and Robert Bauval see an elaborate cosmology presented in the texts, connecting with the star system of Orion. In 1992 when I first saw these texts with Hakim, he stated that the standard translation and interpretations were incomplete and incorrect. I will return to these texts in Part Three of this book.

In our on-site investigations with Hakim, there was one particular area which he continually focused on. North of the Step Pyramid is an area which I believe was an ancient lake perhaps filled by some of the tunnels bringing water from the west, the ancient Ur Nil. There is a mound in the center of this dried-up lake bed where Hakim holds meditations to connect with the energy of the site. On the mound I found distinct evidence of ritual offerings, pottery and bone chips and remnants of burnt grains, obviously an area of sacred pilgrimage for many thousands of years. The indigenous tradition states this mound was the site of an original Per-Ba, of which very little evidence remains. It is in this area where Hakim has continually demonstrated his ability to open the energy of the site. In 1997, Hakim put me in an altered state of consciousness while in meditation, and I was able "to see" the entire area as it was well over 10,000 years ago. I could see the ancient Per-Ba on a small islet with a lake all around it and lush greenery in all the surrounding areas. My continual impressions every time I return to this area have been that the lake and mound were the focal point of many continued pilgrimages to this site that was considered sacred throughout dynastic Khemitian history. This is another area where I believe rigorous excavations would reveal many more structures under the sand.

I cannot leave the site of Sakkara without some commentary on the Serapeum. A mile or so northwest of the Step Pyramid can be found one of the most amazing areas in all of Egypt, an elaborate underground system of chambers known as the Serapeum. It was so named by the Greeks relating to the sacred Apis bull, and for the Neter, *Serapis* (derived from

Osiris-Apis).[3] In the chambers are large stone boxes called *sarcophagus* by Egyptologists (stone enclosures for coffins, literally means "body-eater" in Greek) that are believed to be for the bodies of sacrificed bulls. Almost all the boxes are made of huge pieces of granite, except a singular one of basalt. It is estimated the lids alone weigh about 35 tons and each whole box over 100 tons. How they could have been carved and lowered into the narrow chamber spaces has not been adequately addressed by Egyptologists. The date attributed to the Serapeum by Egyptologists is from the 18th Dynasty of the New Kingdom Period (ca. 1500-1300 BC), based on some pottery shard founds on the floor (not in the boxes) which is purely arbitrary with no real hard evidence to support it.

It has been proposed by Christopher Dunn that the granite and basalt boxes could have been carved only by advanced machining techniques and not by hand with copper or bronze tools. Furthermore, Dunn states that the stone boxes had to have been carved and finished *in situ*, meaning in the narrow chambers themselves. If they had been finished above ground, the temperature and humidity difference in the underground chambers would have altered their shape and they might not have fit so perfectly in their respective alcoves.[4] The precision of all the surfaces would have been altered if they had been carved above ground and then moved into the underground alcoves. We (Bob Vawter and myself) estimated only five to eight people could have fit comfortably in the narrow chamber areas in which the boxes sit, and it would have been impossible to carve the boxes by the hand methods (copper chisels) believed by Egyptologists. The indigenous tradition dates the Serapeum to thousands of years before dynastic Khemit. They were not sarcophagi for sacrificed bulls, but perhaps they were used for creating acoustic harmonic resonance, with flowing water nearby and underneath. No evidences of mummified bulls has ever been found in the stone boxes, but Egyptologists steadfastly adhere to this explanation nonetheless.

Lastly I return to the Step Pyramid complex to introduce an indigenous Khemitian teaching about the purpose and function of some of the structures. As mentioned, I believe the enclosure was built many thousands of years before the Step Pyramid and was much more important to the ancient Khemitians than the Per-Ka that became the pyramid. Around the courtyard there are many fragments of alabaster lying in the now all desert sand floor (*see* Figure 37). The courtyard floor was originally all covered with alabaster, a crystal used for transmission of sound energy. The indigenous tradition states that at Sakkara one of the main uses of sound was for healing. Hakim maintains this is why the great physician priest Imhotep worked in this area, that he was the last of those ancient masters who knew and taught these techniques, and this is the reason why the later dynastic Khemitians deified him and the Greeks equated him with Ascelepius, their God of Medicine. It is this principle of working with sound, acoustical harmonic resonance, that was one of the true purposes of the Per-Neters and Per-Bas as espoused by the indigenous Khemitian teachings.

Figure 37.
Sakkara. Step Pyramid with courtyard in foreground. Now all sand,
the courtyard floor was once all
made of alabaster and may
be much older than the
Step Pyramid. 1999.
Photo by author.

CHAPTER NINE

ABUSIR AND
ABU GHUROB

ABOUT TWO MILES north of Sakkara lie the dual sites of Abusir and Abu Ghurob. Abusir in Arabic means "Father of Sardines," which does not make any sense as there has not been any significant water source for fish in the area for many thousands of years. Abd'El Hakim points out, however, that Abusir is directly derived from the Khemitian term Bu Wizzer, and that this site may have been the center or capitol of the ancient Bu Wizzer civilization.

At Abusir are found the remnants of several structures, pyramids and temples, and other features. On the basis of their translations of inscriptions found in the area over 100 years ago, Egyptologists date the site to the 5th Dynasty of the Old Kingdom period (ca. 2450 BC). They see the area as an extended necropolis of Sakkara and a burial site for kings. But as at Sakkara and Dahshur (and every Bu Wizzer site I will mention), no actual mummy or body has ever been found in an ancient Per-Neter that was an original burial.

The indigenous Khemitian tradition relates that Abusir is a very old site and the Per-Neters and Per-Bas found there in ruins are much older than the dynastic Khemitian dates assigned to them. First of all, the inscriptions found there (mistranslated to begin with) may have been added thousands of years after the original constructions, so would not be original. We found distinct evidence for many water channels and remnants of ancient lake beds at the site. Presently a lake called Abusir Lake still exists east of the site and Egyptologists believe it was formed from the present Nile River. However, we found some extinct lake beds and ancient water channels west of Abusir Lake to indicate the present lake may be all that remains of a much more extensive system of lakes and canals going west to east, from the ancient Ur Nil.

We spent time investigating the remains of a Per-Neter and surrounding structures attributed to a king with the title *Sahura* (ca. 2440 BC).[1] Instead of seeing a pyramid as a tomb for a king and mortuary temples and other structures as part of a funerary complex, we arrived at very different conclusions. Tracing an ancient lake bed to the complex, we found limestone channels leading to an area in front of the Per-Neter that was not a funerary complex at all. The area in front of the Per-Neter had basalt floors with granite walls and appeared to be a series of docks for boats (*see* Figure 38). We found remnants of aqueducts coming from the lake bed to this area and channels for water all around. The most revealing evidence was that the area sloped downward from west to east for the water to flow in that direction (*see* Figure 39). As the present Nile River is eight to ten miles east of the site, these water courses did not seem to have been built for the current river, but from a water source in the western desert, the ancient Ur Nil.

The water channels seemed to go under the Per-Neter, indicating that possibly the Per-Neter was built after the aqueducts and water channels and was involved with the water in some way. The use of the igneous rock, basalt and granite was not because of a king's whim, but for real, practical, geophysical reasons, perhaps for harmonic acoustical resonance. The interactions of the water and the igneous rock was obviously intentional and has formed a major basis for our conclusions as to the purposes of the Per-Neters.

Figure 38.
Abusir. Near Pyramid of Sahura. Granite column
has cartouche of *Sahura* at top. Abd'El Hakim
believes inscriptions were carved thousands of
years after column was made. Hakim (left) stands
in area of ancient docks made of basalt and granite. 1997. Photo by author.

We took further soil samples near the Sahura complex and found
more evidence of silt under the top layer of sand and also again found
watermarks on sand dunes to indicate there once was extensive water present at this site. We found further evidence of varied styles of pottery,
some thrown by hand perhaps before the invention of the wheel, to indicate a pilgrimage site of many thousands of years. We also found thousands of limestone chip fragments of blocks northwest of this complex on

Figure 39.
Abusir. Pyramid of Sahura in background. In foreground are remnants of ancient lake, facing west. Instead of a funerary complex, this appears to be an ancient aqueduct for water. Ground slopes west to east for water source in the west. 1997. Photo by author.

two large sand dunes. Here we also found evidence of water marks, and we have hypothesized the fragments are the remnants of large limestone walls (*see* Figure 40). The walls formed aqueducts for the flow of water to the site. It has been proposed by Mark Lehner that the evidence for docks in front of the Per-Neter of "Sahura" was connected to Abusir Lake east of the site, therefore from the present Nile.[2] However, our observations indicated the water flow was downhill from west to east and could not have possibly been from the current river. I propose Abusir Lake is the remnant of a much larger lake system derived from the ancient Ur Nil, again placing the original structures as being over 10,000 years old.

Abusir remains another of Hakim's favorite areas to visit. Every time I went there with him the children from the surrounding village con-

Figure 40.
Abusir. Abd'El Hakim walking north from Abusir to
Abu Ghurob. Thousands of limestone, granite and
basalt fragments litter the area indicative of a much
more elaborate site. 1997. Photo by author.

stantly mobbed us. Many of these children had green eyes, the distinctive feature of Hakim's ancestral tribe, the Awayanis, the "eye" tribe. The children (and adults) referred to Hakim as "uncle" or "grandpa" to indicate a familial relationship. As at all the Bu Wizzer sites, the guardians of Abusir pay special homage and respect to Abd'El Hakim.

About a mile north from Abusir lies the site of Abu Ghurob. Abu Ghurob translates as "Father of Crow's Nests" in Arabic, and there seems definite justification for this title. There is a large hill where an obelisk once stood and the ruins of a temple complex. From the top of the hill one has a great view both north and south, hence the "crow's nest" appellation (*see* Figure 41). Nothing remains of the obelisk, and the courtyard complex itself is in ruins. Egyptologists see the site as an extension of Abusir, a 5th Dynasty funerary complex for kings.

Figure 41.
Abu Ghurob. Sightline from top of mound where obelisk once stood, facing south. Abusir pyramids can be seen and in distance is Step Pyramid of Sakkara. 1997. Photo by author.

The word obelisk is Greek and refers to a "large spit" (a pointed stick for barbecuing).[3] Obelisks were unique to Khemitian culture and were slender stone structures with pyramidal tops. As it is obvious they were not tombs, Egyptologists define them as representative of the Neter Ra, the sun, and connected them to funerary complexes meant to increase the God's blessings on the dead king. The complex at Abu Ghurob is associated by the Egyptologists with a king titled *Niuserre*, and they call it a "Sun Temple."[4] The Egyptologists see the pyramid complexes as burial centers, and the obelisks and connecting temples as part of the "cult of Ra" and a religious center right next to the funerary complexes.

The indigenous Khemitian tradition tells a very different story. Both Abusir and Abu Ghurob were originally ancient Khemitian ceremonial areas later used by the dynastic peoples as sacred sites. The Khemitian term for obelisk was *Ib Ra*, the "Heart of Ra," a ray of light from the heart of the sun, a sunbeam (*see* Figure 42). The Ib Ra was the power of the sun captured in stone, and granite was the preferable stone to demonstrate the idea. So the Egyptologist's contention of a "new" cult of Ra

Figure 42.
Abu Ghurob. Block of granite with glyphs *Ib Ra*, the Heart of Ra, the Khemitian term for obelisk. 1999. Photo by author.

beginning in the 5th Dynasty is incorrect; it was an attempt by the dynastic peoples to rekindle "that old-time religion." The indigenous tradition states the obelisk and relating structures at Abu Ghurob were ancient already at the time of the 5th Dynasty of the Old Kingdom Period. The obelisk at Abu Ghurob was small by Khemitian standards, 13 to 15 feet high (some have been found up to 150 feet tall), but was one solid piece of granite. Part of a relief we found at the site in May of 1999 indicated the obelisk sat on top of or was connected to a Per-Neter, and both together were part of a system for energy transmission, not in any way constructed to commemorate the memory of an individual king.

A large square structure made of alabaster is in front of the mound where the obelisk stood. It is in the shape of the Khemitian symbol *Hotep*, translated by Egyptologists as "satisfied" or "peace," but also translated by Dr. J. O. Kinnaman as "table of offerings."[5] It is this last translation that seems the most significant here as it seemed obvious to me the structure was an alter for offerings (*see* Figure 43). It may have been an offering table to the Neter Ra or to the "gods," but certainly was not for a dead king! The rounded curves and contoured angles of the alabaster Hotep again indicated the use of sophisticated machining technology and did not appear to have been accomplished by hand with copper chisels (*see* Figure 44). Christopher Dunn agreed with this observation when we were at the site together in May of 1999.

The true uniqueness of this area, however, cannot be appreciated by use of left brain intellectual observation. The greatness of Abd'El Hakim's teachings lies in his ability to open both sides of the brain for people in the field with him, so that they experience heightened awareness at these sites. Hakim had us connect to the energy of the site and use our intuition as well as intellect. Everything about Abu Ghurob seemed very ancient to me, to be much older than many other sites I had investigated. This feeling cannot be quantified, but the energy which spoke of great antiquity combined with the evidence of many structures once standing in this area, now only in ruins, gave an overriding impression of one of the oldest human occupation sites I had ever been at in my

Figure 43.
Abu Ghurob. Alabaster *Hotep*, altar for offerings, in all four directions. 1997. Photo by author.

Figure 44.
Abu Ghurob. Close-up of alabaster *Hotep* showing possible evidence of advanced machining. 1997. Photo by author.

life. Hakim has insisted Abu Ghurob is a very ancient Bu Wizzer area and that the indigenous tradition states the area dates back deep into prehistory.

Several structures still remaining at this site are also the subject of controversy. On several occasions we have studied several square pieces of alabaster with unusual gear-like designs on top (*see* Figure 45). Egyptologists have labeled these structures "basins" because they have indentations on the top. German Egyptologist Ludwig Borchardt theorized these structures were used for ritual sacrifices of animals, but there is no evidence such as bones or blood stains to support this idea.[6] The "basins" exhibit evidence of circular tool marks of sophisticated machining used by the ancient Khemitians to polish and contour angles in alabaster, granite and basalt (*see* Figure 46).

None of the Egyptologists have ventured a theory as to why there are gear-like spokes at the top of these "basins." We would suggest that they were carved for a definite purpose, that something was meant to attach to these structures and rotate or spin. According to the indigenous tradition, these structures were never created for animal sacrifices, but that the alabaster was used for its vibratory, energetic qualities.

Abu Ghurob is a site that must be experienced to fully appreciate its importance. Hakim has always emphasized its importance to me as he believes it to be one of the oldest occupation or ceremonial sites in all Khemit, if not the whole planet. There is no doubt it was a very sacred site to the Khemitians, both to the ancient and dynastic people, who constantly returned there on pilgrimages for apparent ritualistic reasons. Alabaster, as well as granite, basalt and limestone, was used extensively in the area to create physical as well as spiritual effects through the use of vibrations which opened the senses and stimulated heightened awareness to "communicate" directly with the Neters. The indigenous tradition teaches that the Neters themselves, in some sort of physical form, once "landed" and appeared in person at Abu Ghurob. This is why the Khemitians venerated and returned to this site for thousands of years in sacred pilgrimage. The alabaster, granite, basalt and limestone created a

Figure 45.
Abu
Ghurob.
Abd'El
Hakim
examining
one of the
alabaster
"basins."
Note the
strange
gear-like
design
around top.
1997.
Photo by
author.

Figure 46.
Abu Ghurob. Side
of one of the
alabaster "basins."
Tape marks are to
indicate circular
polish marks that
may suggest ultra-
sonic advanced
machining. 1997.
Photo by author.

harmonic resonance through sound vibrations to increase the heightened awareness and to further open the senses to "communicate" and be one with the Neters. These are the teachings of the indigenous Khemitian tradition, that these sites were used to benefit all the people, the Sesh, not for the service solely of royalty as their burial places.

CHAPTER TEN

ZAWIYET EL ARYAN

ABOUT THREE OR four miles north of Abu Ghurob and about two miles south of Giza lies the small village of Zawiyet el Aryan. Zawiyet means "angle" in Arabic, and Aryan was the name of a famous Coptic Christian priest. The area is also referred to as Zawiyet el Musalim, "The Angle of the Muslims." There are remnants of several structures in this area, including what has been called the Layer Pyramid, attributed to the 3rd Dynasty of the Old Kingdom period (ca. 2600 BC). There is another pyramid at this site considered to be from the end of the 4th Dynasty.[1]

Hakim had insisted that Zawiyet was an important area to investigate, that there was something specific he wanted to show. He had remembered many pyramids and ruins of related structures of great antiquity being there from when he was young. But Hakim had not been to this area in many years, and the village, having gotten much larger, covered much of the ruins he wanted to show Bob Vawter and myself. It was clear there was a certain spot he wanted us to see but could not find exactly where it was. We drove all through this small village and spent a whole day trying to locate it. For the most part, the local villagers were friendly towards us, but we would not disturb their living areas. It might have seemed like we were wasting our time driving around this small village, but we knew to trust Hakim's desire to show us something important to the whole Bu Wizzer paradigm of older structures. We waited in the car while Hakim consulted the local elders. When at last he returned, he informed us that the area in question now had a mosque built on top of it.

In the center of the village is the mosque built on top of a Coptic Christian church, which was built on top of a dynastic Khemitian temple. This is a familiar theme found throughout Egypt (and the whole planet). This was an example of Hakim's teaching of the "layering" of different structures from various time periods in Khemitian history and prehistory. Later generations or civilizations venerate sacred sites of previous peoples, so they build their religious shrines on sites long ago chosen by the ancients for the energy present. I believe the dynastic Khemitians built their temple on top of an even older Khemitian structure that was from the Bu Wizzer civilization. The energy in this area was very powerful. When we attempted to approach the mosque and take some pictures, some fundamentalist Muslims grew uneasy and formed a phalanx to block the entrance to the gate. The friendly attitude towards us dissipated, and we were not allowed to fully investigate this site. It was obvious the people considered the area to be sacred, and we did not want to push the point. We sat in the car for a while and meditated. We all felt the powerful energy present was indicative of something very important on the site.

In later discussions about this area, Hakim reiterated his belief that the mosque was built over an ancient energy place known to the ancient Khemitians. He felt the center of the mosque was on top of the "Holy of Holies," the central power spot of an ancient Per-Ba. He continued to emphasize that the spot was a major energy vortex known to the ancient Khemitians and an essential point of focus for all the Bu Wizzer sites.

Researcher Larry Hunter having done some detailed investigations of Zawiyet in the last few years has stated he has discovered evidence of older structures under the pyramid ruins of larger, more massive blocks of limestone and granite, evidence I believe of the ancient Khemitian methods and style of architecture. In a small, independently produced pamphlet entitled "Project Gateway to Orion," Hunter and his partner, Alex Knott, published their research results, that the remains of the alleged 3rd Dynasty pyramid, the Layer Pyramid, was built of small stones and appeared to be a step pyramid, as at Sakkara. Surrounding these remains, in the outlying sand dunes, they found evidence of large, limestone blocks like those at Giza and Dahshur. They stated that the small blocks of the so-called Layer Pyramid were a brownish color while the larger eroded limestone blocks in the sand dunes were the white color seen at Giza. Hunter and Knott concluded that the larger, more eroded limestone blocks must represent a construction of an older timeframe than the Layer Pyramid. These observations coincided with our conclusions from the other sites already mentioned, that the dynastic Khemitians built their structures on top of or near the ruins of ancient Khemitian buildings.

In his book, *The Ancient Secret of the Flower of Life*, Drunvalo Melchizedek spoke of an area he visited near Sakkara where he was shown the ruins of a pyramid called "Lehirit."[2] Drunvalo mentioned many other pyramids in this area located on military installations. Drunvalo stated he was told the pyramid of "Lehirit" was much older than the Step Pyramid of Sakkara. As there are military installations west of Sakkara, Abusir and Zawiyet el Aryan, I believe Drunvalo was taken to ruins outside the village of Zawiyet. Drunvalo mentioned being taken through a small village to find the ruins he spoke of and it being a half an hour from Sakkara. This definitely sounds like Zawiyet el Aryan, and Drunvalo was apparently shown ruins of ancient Khemitian structures. When I discussed this with Hakim, he said he had never heard of "Lehirit" but stated that the area Drunvalo described sounded like the ruins west of Zawiyet.

We did not get a chance to fully investigate the structures present in the entire area surrounding the village of Zawiyet el Aryan. With the apparent importance of the spot the mosque is built over and the extensive ruins still on military installations, much more investigative work needs to be accomplished in this area.

GIZA

THE AREA OF the Giza Plateau is by far the most famous archaeological site in the world. Located over 20 miles north of Dahshur, about eight miles west of modern Cairo, Giza (pronounced Gee-zah) means "skirt" in Arabic, meant to describe the whole plateau, which is the home of nine pyramids, three large, six small, the Great Sphinx, and numerous shaft tombs cut into the limestone bedrock (*see* Figure 47).

Giza also can be the most difficult site in which to undertake serious investigations, being the busiest and noisiest in the daytime, visited daily by thousands of tourists and populated by hundreds of hawkers, camel jockeys, antiquities police, military, undercover police, local villagers and amateur archaeologists. Many of the most serious excavations have been conducted after hours or at night. Yet, it is also the area where we have conducted our most extensive research, having the great privilege to have walked the site many hours in the presence of Abd'El Hakim. His village, Nazlet el Samman, nestles right at the foot of the Giza Plateau.

It is from Giza, more than any other place, that the whole of

Figure 47.
Giza. The Great Sphinx, as I first saw her. 1992.
Photo by author.

Egyptology derives its main paradigms. I have mentioned the writings of the Greeks Herodotus and Manetho who provided the view that the pyramids and temples were built to service a religion based on the resurrection of dead kings' souls. Egyptologists recognize the pyramids of Giza as tombs for royalty and nothing more. The Giza site is believed to have been settled and created as a necropolis during the 4th Dynasty of the Old Kingdom period (ca. 2500 BC). The archaeological evidence supports some of this view as there was definitely a cemetery on the site and many burials during this time, which is the main evidence rendered by Egyptologists to support the Greek paradigm. Yet no evidence of a burial has ever been found in any of the Giza pyramids, a fact that is explained away as being the result of pernicious tomb robberies.

The orthodox view is that the Giza Plateau was a deserted, rocky area

108

at the beginning of the 4th Dynasty of the Old Kingdom period (ca. 2600 BC). Supposedly, the second king of this dynasty, named *Khnum-Khuf* or *Khufu* (called *Suphis*, then later *Cheops* by the Greeks), decided to locate in this area and have a pyramid built for his tomb. Later, his third son, named *Khafra*, had a smaller pyramid built nearby, on higher ground so the two pyramids would appear equal in height. He (Khafra, called *Chephren* by the Greeks) then had a limestone outcropping carved into the Great Sphinx with his likeness for its face. Khafra's son, named *Menkaura* (*Mykerinos* to the Greeks), built the third and smallest pyramid near the other two. All their nobles and servants were also buried near their kings. Then the site was abandoned and the next dynasty of kings built their pyramids at Sakkara and Abusir.[1]

The indigenous tradition of Egypt offers a very different interpretation and explanation of the Giza structures. These differences have already been voiced, specifically that a Per-Neter was not a tomb for a king (or anyone). New York City Police Detective Frank Domingo, a forensic artist and member of John Anthony West's research team, sufficiently challenged and refuted the claim that the face of the Sphinx is the same as found on a statue with the title Khafra. By using the techniques of biometric analysis, that is measuring angles and distances between the eyes, nose and chin of both a photograph of the face of the Sphinx and of a statue with the cartouche of Khafra, Detective Domingo was very clear in stating that the face of the Sphinx and the one on the statue of Khafra were not of the same individual (*see* Figure 48).[2] Moreover, the indigenous tradition states that the supposed names of these kings were not names at all, but titles that may have been held by many different kings, so we may not be able to determine who exactly Khufu or Khafra were.

In fact, another indigenous teacher, Mayan Daykeeper Hunbatz Men, has provided a clue to a different meaning for the terms *Khnum-Khuf* or *Khufu*. As mentioned, I shared a brief correspondence with Mr. Men in 1997. At that time he stated, "it turns out to be that K'UFU is the real name of the pyramid of KEOPS. K'U means GOD in Maya Itza [language] or *sacred area* [italics mine]."[3] Many times Hakim asserted to me that the "names" Khufu, Khafra and Menkaura were titles that referred to a particular connection to a Neter and could have been applied to many kings, or that they may have actually been titles of the Per-Neters themselves, or as Hunbatz has stated, to the sacred area of the Giza Plateau.

My research and observations have indicated a totally different story

Figure 48.
Giza. Profile of the Sphinx. I concur with Detective Frank Domingo that this is not the same face as that on the statue of King Khafra in the Cairo Museum. 1997. Photo by author.

than that of the Egyptologists. The Giza Plateau is literally honey-combed with underground tunnels. Egyptologists have never adequately attempted to explain why and how these tunnels were constructed, except to incorporate them in their pyramid-as-tomb paradigms. They propose these tunnels were used as "trial runs" for the later passages in the pyramids, for practice drilling or for "swimming pools." It has also been suggested by some Egyptologists that these tunnels were for "symbolic tombs" of the Gods, etc.[4] They also propose these tunnels were drilled or carved with the same copper chisels that they claim were used to cut the limestone and granite for the pyramids. As one who has investigated some of these tunnels personally and seen the right angles cut through solid bedrock with relatively smooth walls, any explanation of these tunnels being cut with anything other than advanced machining techniques seems blatantly absurd (*see* Figure 49). Again, being in the field at Giza in May of 1999 with Christopher Dunn, we were able to confirm our observations and add more support to his theories that advanced machining had to have been employed to cut these tunnels and build the pyramids.

The indigenous tradition clearly states that the main purposes of the underground tunnels was to bring water to the Giza Plateau. My observations and investigations of both the tunnels underneath the Giza Plateau and the obvious water channels on the surface of the site indicated a water flow from the south and west, which would not be from the current Nile River, located eight miles or more east of Giza. The whole Giza Plateau slopes downward from west to east.

Many Egyptologists have suggested the Nile in the 4th Dynasty was further west than it is today (although still to the east of the plateau) and that would account for the presence of water channels and a possible lake in front of the Sphinx. But our observations indicated the water flowed downhill from west to east and could not have been from an eastern source, but from a western one, the ancient Ur Nil (*see* Figure 50). Some of the shafts on the plateau have been estimated to lead straight down 300 meters (over 1,000 feet) by Hakim, and it would have required a tremen-

Figure 49.
Giza. Inside one of the tunnels underneath the
Plateau. Notice relatively smooth walls and right
angles cut right through limestone bedrock. 1997.
Photo by author.

Figure 50.
Giza Plateau, facing south. Notice downward
slope of limestone bedrock, west to east, for water
to flow to Sphinx hollow.
1999. Photo by author.

dous effort to drill through the limestone bedrock. Also, we observed some of the tunnels may extend for miles and further investigation could confirm Hakim's boyhood story. It would seem ridiculous to cut miles of underground tunnels and then flood the site if it was primarily used as a necropolis, a burial place for kings and royalty. The purpose of bringing water to an area is for the living, for agriculture and energy sources, which dead kings would have no use for.

According to the indigenous Khemitian tradition, the tunnels at Giza extend to and throughout all the Bu Wizzer sites. They then extend westward to the ancient Ur Nil. How far westward these tunnels go would take much more extensive and involved investigative work, and without permission from the Egyptian Supreme Council of Antiquities to initiate a serious and involved investigation of the tunnels, this may be nearly impossible to accomplish. These tunnels may extend at least 25-30 miles north to south, and according to tradition, did so well over 10,000 years ago. What seems to be obvious to me is that the ancient Khemitians who drilled these tunnels must have had an extraordinary science and engineering capability. Such a vast project of underground tunnels and aboveground channels and aqueducts must have been undertaken for a real, specific purpose and not just for religious, symbolic reasons.

Christopher Dunn employs this same logic in his book about the Great Pyramid. Observing the incredible accuracy in measurement and construction of the monument and the materials used in and around it, limestone, granite and basalt, Dunn surmised sophisticated science and engineering had to have been employed, and for that enormous an undertaking, a practical as well as spiritual reason had to exist for the structure. He sees the Great Pyramid as a power plant, one of the few theories proposed for the pyramid so far that fits the Khemitian understanding of what a Per-Neter was for. I believe the tunnels and water channels were intrinsically connected to the Great Pyramid and all were constructed during the same era, well over 10,000 years ago. Dunn's theories of the construction methods of and purposes for the Great Pyramid as originally intended agree with not only the indigenous tradition, but with the claims of Dr. J. O. Kinnaman. According to his discoveries inside the pyramid with Sir Flinders Petrie, Dr. Kinnaman stated that one of the purposes of the Great Pyramid was to serve as a giant radio station, to send messages anywhere on the planet. Christopher Dunn states the energy generated in the Great Pyramid could have been emitted as microwave and radio waves, thus supporting the claims of Kinnaman. Other researchers have recently offered theories that propose other functions for the Great Pyramid as an energy device. Ukrainian theoretical physicist Dr. V. Krasnoholovets has recently proposed that the Great Pyramid was built to intentionally amplify basic energy fields of the Earth on a subatomic, quantum level.[5] The synthesis of many varied ideas and theories at this point in time will allow for a more systemic, holistic view of these structures.

Many people mistakenly believe the discovery of the tunnels under the Giza Plateau to be a recent phenomenon. In fact, the tunnels have been known to archaeologists since the 1920s and '30s (and to the Arabs for centuries). American Egyptologist George Reisner excavated a great deal of the Giza Plateau during the 1930s and investigated many of the tunnels. There is a shaft under the causeway behind the Sphinx that is called Reisner's shaft, which is estimated to go down over 1,000 feet and end in water. Hakim, who started his career at age six working for Reisner, has told me that Reisner's son drowned in one of these shafts in the late 1930s, when investigating how far down the tunnels go. Dr. J. O. Kinnaman mentioned in a book about the Great Pyramid he wrote in 1940 that a tunnel leading from the Sphinx to the Great Pyramid had been discovered the previous year, 1938-39, and was to be cleared and investigated. I believe this was when Egyptian Egyptologist Selim Hassan was in charge of excavations around the Sphnix, and was then (late 1930s) searching for hidden chambers and passages under the Sphinx. So the interest in this area has not just arisen in the 1970s, '80s and '90s, but has been ongoing for over 70 years.

The Great Sphinx has been the subject of much debate in the last few years. As I have mentioned, it was R. A. Schwaller de Lubicz who first stated in the late 1950s that the erosion on the body and enclosure of the Sphinx was caused by water, not sand and wind. This theory has been championed by John Anthony West in the last 20 years and supported by Boston University geologist Dr. Robert Schoch. West's book on the subject will be the definitive analysis of their work, but the articles and the aforementioned television special released on video have enabled many of us to challenge the accepted paradigm that the Sphinx was carved 4,500 years ago as being highly inaccurate. The Sphinx has to be older than 7-10,000 years if the massive erosion present on its body and enclosure was the result of extensive and continuous torrential rainfalls (*see* Figure 51). Although it has been argued that occasional flash thunderstorms have occurred in modern and dynastic times, the continuous kind of rainfall

Figure 51.
Giza. Rump of Sphinx and sourthern wall of enclosure showing massive erosion present. 1992. Photo by author.

necessary to cause the erosion seen has not been present in northern Africa for the last 7,000 years or more. Dr. Schoch has adequately addressed both the arguments against his view and the alternative explanations given for the erosion seen.[6]

When I first heard Hakim speak of the Sphinx in November 1992, he calmly asserted that she was over 52,000 years old. Although as an indigenous wisdom keeper Hakim seems never concerned with exact dating and quantification of data, he has always consistently maintained a date of over 50,000 years for the carving of the Sphinx. He has also stated that she was carved first (above ground) before any of the Per-Neters or Per-Bas. Why do we refer to the Sphinx as "She"? This comes from the Khemitian tradition that the Sphinx represents the feminine expression of a Leonine-Human combination, not a masculine one. The Sphinx represents *Tefnut, Sekhmet, Men-Het* and *Mut*—all later expressed by Egyptologists as Lioness Goddesses. In particular, Hakim emphasizes the identification of the Sphinx with Tefnut. The Neter Nut represented the sky, the feminine consciousness of space, and she existed before all material creation. Tefnut is literally translated as "The Spittle of Nut" and represents the first physical manifestation. As Nut "spit" on the Earth, Tefnut manifested and, therefore, the Sphinx was the first created structure at Giza. In the early dynastic periods, the Sphinx was associated with Hathor, still with a feminine connotation. It was only in later periods, such as the 18th Dynasty of the New Kingdom Period (ca. 1500-1100 BC), that there was a patriarchal revision to identify the Sphinx with a male principle, as *Hor-em-akhet*, or "Horus in the Horizon."

Egyptologist Mark Lehner has written that the identification of the Sphinx with the male sun God was prevalent from the 4th Dynasty (2600 BC). He claims the so-called Sphinx and Valley Temples in front of the Sphinx were part of a solar cult, and the Sphinx was supposed to represent the king making offerings to Ra in the temples—a typical patriarchal view based on the Greek paradigm.[7] The indigenous tradition teaches that the structures in front of the Sphinx were not Per-Bas but were constructed as part of the ancient Sphinx complex. Originally, there was a lake surrounding the Sphinx called Lake Hathor by the Khemitians, and the two structures in front were constructed as landing docks, serving as disembarkation points, sort of an ancient customs declaration point. Boats from all over Khemit, and even other lands, would come to the Sphinx and have to "declare" their goods and gifts to her. She was the Guardian of the Plateau, of all the Bu Wizzer sites. The ancient Khemitians also identified the Sphinx with the star system Sirius, and there is no doubt of them seeing the statue in a feminine context. I wrote an article in 1994, published in *World Explorer* magazine, in which I speculated that the face of the Sphinx, as it now appears, was that of a Black African female (*see* Figure 52). I offered evidence that the first male king of the dynastic period, ca. 3100 BC, who had the title *Hor-Aha*, may have had the face of the Sphinx recarved to resemble that of his mother, *Neith-Hotep*, and she may have been a Black African. Race was unimportant to the Khemitians, but tribal identity and matrilineal lineage were, so this

Figure 52.
Giza. Profile of the Sphinx. Is this the face of a Black African female? 1999. Photo by author.

king may have intended to venerate his descent by honoring his mother.

Hakim has also pointed out that the causeway behind the Sphinx presents some problems for the accepted paradigms. According to the orthodox chronology, King Khafra had the middle pyramid constructed as his tomb, then had the causeway constructed, then the Sphinx carved. But the actual layout belies this chronology. The Sphinx sits in her own hollow, excavated out when she was carved, and the blocks were then used to construct the structures in front of her. But the causeway coming from the middle Per-Neter does not go directly to the back of the Sphinx, but rather at an angle to the side of her. This obviously shows the Sphinx was carved first and the Per-Neter and causeway constructed many years after. The causeway is composed of limestone artificially added to the bedrock, and therefore is hollow and lies over the water tunnels.

Hakim has also emphatically stated that the middle pyramid, not constructed by any king, was the first Per-Neter built on the Giza Plateau (*see* Figure 53). He supports this by saying the middle pyramid, as the first Per-Neter, was constructed on a mound, the highest point on the Plateau. Interestingly enough, there is some supporting evidence from the academic Egyptologists themselves for Hakim's declarations of the middle pyramid being the first Per-Neter. John Baines and Jaromir Malek have stated that the middle pyramid was known in ancient times as "The Great Pyramid," and the current Great Pyramid had another title.[8] This statement may have come from the indigenous sources as recorded by Baines and Malek, clearly indicating that the middle pyramid predated the Great Pyramid at the Giza site. The reason the pyramid was constructed on top of a mound, not leveled in the middle, was to fuse with the Earth and to serve as a seismic tap, resonating and harmonizing with basic Earth vibration. Christopher Dunn wrote in his book that the Great Pyramid served a similar purpose, resonating and vibrating in acoustical resonant harmony with the Earth's natural vibration. Dunn, therefore, referred to the Great Pyramid as a coupled oscillator, vibrating in harmony with the Earth's basic vibratory rate.[9] I believe the middle pyramid, the first Per-Neter, is a basic seismic tap, amplifying and

Figure 53.
Giza. The middle pyramid, called Khafra.
There is a tradition stating that this was the first
pyramid constructed at Giza. 1999. Photo by
author.

resonating to the Earth's energy, and the Great Pyramid was later built in
resonant frequency with the middle pyramid to further amplify the
harmonic resonance and utilize this energy. The role water played in the
process will need its own chapter for full explanation, but for here I will

state the experiments and investigations I did with Bob Vawter and Abd'El Hakim have led me to conclude all the Per-Neters of Bu Wizzer acted together in acoustical harmonic resonance.

There are many researchers who are in the process of mapping the actual acoustical frequencies of all the Bu Wizzer Per-Neters. I believe each Per-Neter was "tuned" to a different frequency and they then resonated together for an overall holistic harmony, symbolized by the Khemitians by the glyph *Nefer*, not merely meaning "beauty" as translated by the Egyptologists, but "Harmony," a much more profound meaning. We have made sound recordings in some of the Per-Neters, testing the frequencies, but much more work is yet to be done. Acoustical engineer Thomas Danley has also done some pivotal work in the Great Pyramid, mapping sound frequencies, and is also convinced it was constructed to utilize acoustic harmonic resonance.[10] The hope is to continue the research in this area to create a coherent, dynamic paradigm to encompass the full functions and reasons for the construction of the Bu Wizzer Per-Neters.

In the hours of investigation and observation on the Giza Plateau with Hakim, he has pointed out many things to support the indigenous Khemitian tradition. In front of the First Per-Neter, the middle pyramid, is what the Egyptologists label a mortuary temple supposedly built for King Khafra. But through the eyes of an indigenous master, this structure is seen to not have been a Per-Ba, but a great passageway for the water to flow from the Per-Neter to the Sphinx lake. One can see huge "shoulders" constructed of massive slabs of limestone to form a great lintel, a passageway for water to flow through (*see* Figure 54). These were "docks" for boats to pass through to the Per-Neter. I have also observed huge pavement stones in front of the Per-Neters, stones that may weigh over 100 tons, some in the shape of rectangles over 30 feet long on their longest sides. Also, on the eastern side of the Great Pyramid are pavement stones of basalt, laid on top of the limestone pavement stones (*see* Figure 55). Why this was done has never been addressed by Egyptologists, but I believe it was for increased resonance, the basalt vibrating in harmony with the limestone. The source for the vibration was the water coursing underneath, a theme I will elaborate upon.

The indigenous tradition also tells us that although there are nine pyramids on the Giza Plateau, originally there were a greater number. We have done some preliminary investigation of an area a short distance from the smallest, third pyramid that may be the remains of another pyramid that has been completely quarried. There may be yet another pyramid still buried under the sand south of this area. Much more investigative work needs to be done to verify this aspect of the tradition.

On Tuesday, March 2, 1999, the Fox Television Network broadcast a live show from the Giza Plateau. It was a monumentous undertaking and the broadcast aspect of the show was a tremendous success. The show featured Dr. Zahi Hawass, Undersecretary of State for the Giza Plateau, and followed a format that "live archaeology" would be shown to the world. As far as presenting real archaeology, the show fell short of expectations. It was obviously a staged event of presenting "actual" finds, and I personally received many phone calls and e-mails from archaeologists and other friends quite upset at what was presented.

I do hope, however, that the show would encourage and inspire people to go to Egypt to see the evidence for themselves and to greatly increase tourism, on which the Egyptian people so sorely depend. But as for adding evidence and support for the orthodox theories, Zahi Hawass accomplished the opposite, instead adding support for our new Khemitological paradigms. I will discuss the three "finds" in this light. The first, the alleged "find" of an actual mummy, was rife with contradictions. Digging in the western cemetery—to the west of the Great Pyramid where a definite 4th Dynasty necropolis exists—Hawass claimed he had found a tomb "related" to a high priest named Kai. Hawass stated on the Fox special that the tomb "must be a relative" of Kai as his name was found in outer inscriptions.

But, upon entering the tomb and removing the wooden coffin in three neat, easy pieces (obviously staged), Hawass announced, without any detailed examination, that the almost pristine mummy laying there

Figure 54.
Giza. Structures in front of middle pyramid. Abd'El Hakim sees these as passageways for boats over 10,000 years ago. 1999. Photo by author.

Figure 55.
Giza. Eastern side of Great Pyramid showing remains of huge basalt stones on top of limestone pavement stones. 1992. Photo by author.

was of the High Priest Kai himself! How could he have possibly known that? Then Hawass stated the mummy was not from the 4th Dynasty, but possibly from the First Intermediate Period and was approximately 4,200 years old (300 years later than the 4th Dynasty dates)—so the mummy could not possibly be that of Kai. Hawass could not know all this unless the mummy had already been found and tested. Even so, if it was 300 years later than the 4th Dynasty, then it was not an original burial, but a later intrusive one. As mentioned, an intrusive burial is one in which a later group of people, wishing to be identified with an earlier, venerated people, have themselves buried in the monuments and structures of the earlier people in order to be somehow connected with them. I maintain any burial found in the real Per-Neters, the original Bu Wizzer and ancient Khemitian Per-Neters and Per-Bas, are all intrusive burials, as they were never originally intended as burial (Per-Ka) sites. The dynastic Khemitians turned all the inactive Bu Wizzer sites into necropoli in order to identify with the legendary, almost mythical, ancients.

The second "find" of Hawass was even more extraordinary. Hawass and Mark Lehner are the recognized champions of the orthodox paradigms of Egyptology of pyramids-as-tombs, and the pyramids being nothing more than that. Hawass took live television viewers into one of the small pyramids near the third pyramid, supposedly built by the King Menkaura. The pyramid was supposed to be the tomb of one of the king's "wives," his sister who had the title, *Khamerenebty*. In actuality, she was the Per-Aa, the High House, and was the reason her brother had his status, but be that as it may, we were told this "small" pyramid was built as her tomb. I actually got a little nervous as it appeared Hawass had found some great evidence to support his paradigms, but was amazed when he had to admit in front of the whole world that the "burial chamber" was unfinished, the stone box (sarcophagus) empty, and no one was ever buried there! We were all pleased how Hawass had inadvertently given so much support to the indigenous tradition that no one was ever buried in a true Per-Neter.

The last "find" was the most significant and powerful for us and our work. Claiming he had found the "Tomb of Osiris," Hawass unveiled an amazing sight to the world. In a central chamber area over 100 feet down into the limestone bedrock of the Giza Plateau, Zahi Hawass and Fox cameras unveiled a great sight. What was not told to the audience was that this area had been located years ago and had been submerged in water. It had taken several years of pumping to clear the chamber, and this was done in 1997-98. Hawass and his team had found a stone box ("sarcophagus") in a central pool of water completely empty. They had already looked inside at least a year before, so when Hawass had the lid lifted for the cameras, it was again a staged opening. He announced this was the "Tomb of Osiris," but showed no concrete evidence for this conclusion.[11] My conclusions were that this was more evidence for the tunnels and the whole Giza Plateau not being originally constructed as a necropolis, for burials.

The interest for me was the myriad of tunnels that led to this central location, like the spokes of a wheel leading to the center shaft. Were they all water tunnels, channeling into this area for a specific reason? I believe the answer is yes, and I will return to explain why when we discuss the role of the water in the whole Per-Neter process and the purpose of all the water tunnels, channels and aqueducts. It is enough to state here that Zahi Hawass provided great support for the new paradigms and not the outdated, inadequate orthodox theories. Hawass did not even begin to try to explain how all those tunnels could have been made over 100 feet down into the limestone bedrock—and we have found evidence the tunnels may go down over 1,000 feet.

In discussing the Fox special with several colleagues, we all agreed that the show amplified Hakim's basic teaching of the Khemitian belief that a new Dawn of Consciousness is coming, and no matter what the Egyptologists, or anyone, tries to promote or obfuscate, the Truth will be known once again.

Zahi Hawass stated on the Fox show, and has said in print many times, that Egyptologists have only excavated less than 20 percent of all there is under the Giza Plateau. In this I totally agree, and know much more will be uncovered in the next few years. All researchers hope it will be shown and revealed totally to the whole world.

CHAPTER TWELVE

ABU ROASH

 LAST BUT CERTAINLY not least of the Bu Wizzer sites is Abu Roash. Located about five miles northwest of Giza, Abu Roash was the northern border of Bu Wizzer but would have been placed at the bottom of a Khemitian map, following the flow of the river, south to north. Abu Roash means "Father of Cooks" in Arabic, and the reason for this name remains obscure.

The orthodox view of Abu Roash proposes an elaborate story. Egyptologists claim that a son of Khufu, named *Djedefra* (not his eldest son, *Kawit* or *Kawab*, of whom there is no evidence of his ever building anything), left the Giza complex where his father had the greatest pyramid in the world built (according to their theories) to move five miles to Abu Roash. Egyptologists only speculate on why he did this, perhaps because of rivalry with his other brothers (Khafra who would succeed him), and so he began the construction of a pyramid at Abu Roash which he did not finish.

The only evidence linking Djedefra to Abu Roash were the remains of a king's head carved in dark purple quartzite found in some rubble near the site. A cartouche found with the head had the title Djedefra, so it was then assumed this was an individual who had the pyramid constructed for his tomb. Egyptologists state the style of the structure is a throwback to the 3rd Dynasty pyramids and is quite inferior compared to the Great Pyramid.[1] The pyramid was built on a small hill and would only have been about 190 feet tall if it had been completed, and is estimated to have been 348 feet to a side. When compared to the Great Pyramid which is 484 feet high (with capstone added, 454 feet high as it stands today) and 755 feet to a side, this pyramid would appear minuscule. Why would the son, having become king and with the same resources, material and manpower available to him as his father, have chosen to build such an inferior monument to himself?

Of course it should be obvious by now I do not accept any of the preceding chronology and explanation by Egyptologists. According to the indigenous tradition, Abu Roash was an ancient Bu Wizzer site and the pyramid was not incomplete. The hill on which the pyramid was built was more than 100 feet higher than the Giza Plateau, and this elevation would have provided a great sight line to the south as the northern border site. There is no real evidence linking this site to the 4th Dynasty or any other timeframe in the Old Kingdom dynastic period.

My on-site observations of Abu Roash were very interesting. First of all, there are no antiquities police, no ticket vendors, no hawkers and no tourists at this site. Mark Lehner has stated that excavations were undertaken by a Franco-Swiss team in 1995, but I saw no evidence of any recent excavations when I was there in 1997. The site seemed virtually deserted, and there was no one else there to interfere with my and Hakim's investigations. We were able to locate the "socket" stones marking the pyramid's layout and to find the pavement stones (see Figure 56). We also saw many remnants of granite blocks to indicate the ancient Bu Wizzer construction style of the Khemitians (see Figure 57). Egyptologists do not comment on how they could have hauled thousands of tons of limestone and granite hundreds of feet up the hill to build the pyramid.

Figure 56.
Abu Roash. Author
locating pavement
stones of pyramid.
1997. Photo by
Abd'El Hakim Awyan.

Figure 57.
Abu Roash.
Evidence of
granite blocks
used in pyramid.
1997. Photo by
author.

Our observations indicated the small mountain was "cored out" in order to construct the Per-Neter inside. We found evidence of the core stones still "married" or fused to the limestone bedrock of the hill, and I concluded with Hakim the pyramid was not left incomplete but had been a full, functional Per-Neter in its time by virtue of the fact the infrastructure stones were still in place (*see* Figure 58). To be in the ruinous state it is today, it has been either quarried or partially destroyed. We were able to descend the 100 feet or so into the hill, and I was interested to observe the smooth walls of the hollowed out hill that reminded me of the inside of the tunnels I had entered at Giza and observed at Sakkara (*see* Figure 59). It seemed apparent to me the same people who drilled the tunnels at Giza and Sakkara also cored out this hill and built the Per-Neter at Abu Roash (*see* Figure 60).

At the top of the hill we were able to enjoy a fantastic sightline to the south; we could see the Giza pyramids, and on a clear day without smog from Cairo, we could probably have seen to Sakkara (*see* Figure 61). Perhaps when originally built, one could see all the way to the Dahshur

Figure 58.
Abu Roash. Infrastructure stones of pyramid
"fused" with natural limestone. Photo by author.

pyramids, some 25 miles to the south. The original casing stones covering the sides of the pyramids, gleaming brightly in the sun, would have made them much more visible than they are today. It definitely appeared to us the Bu Wizzer sites were all aligned on some yet undiscovered grid line, and this lent credence to the indigenous tradition that they were all planned at the same relative time period and by the same people, the ancient Khemitians.

Visiting all the Bu Wizzer sites in 1997, one after the other from south to north, was an amazing experience. I was able to see the thread, the connective links in all the areas that opened up my mind and senses to experience a brief glimpse into what had been a great civilization. The final links were forged in November 1998 when Hakim and I took another incredible journey into the field to find the ancient source of the civilization of Khemit.

Figure 59.
Abu Roash. Further view of infrastructure stones from bottom of hollowed-out core of pyramid. 1997. Photo by author.

Figure 60.
Abu Roash. Hollowed-out hill with some core
blocks still evident. Local village boy for scale.
1997. Photo by author.

Figure 61.
Abu Roash. Sightline from top of pyramid hill.
Giza pyramids in distance and faint pyramid at
Abusir. 1997. Photo by author.

CHAPTER THIRTEEN

THE UR NIL
AND THE OASES

 VEN BEFORE RECEIVING the teaching of an older Nile located in the Western Desert of Egypt from Hakim in 1997, I had been familiar with the concept from the book *Egypt Before the Pharaohs* by American Egyptologist Michael Hoffman first written in 1979. I had been given a copy as a gift by a Rosicrucian friend, Charles Jacob, in early 1992 before I made my first trip to Egypt that fall. Charlie has since passed on to a higher plane, but he always encouraged me not to let anyone or anything prevent me from completing this work. In his book, Hoffman discussed the geology of Northern Africa as investigated by many geologists who had studied the area.

One particular section of Hoffman's book stuck in my mind as he stated, "At the turn of the century, a German scientist, M. L. P. Blanckenhorn, speculated that a huge ancestral Nile of tremendous volume—an Ur Nil he called it—once flowed to the west of the present river. He based his conclusions in part on the occurrence of ancient gravels in the Western Desert. For years he was disbelieved. Now, scholarly opinion, like a great, slow-moving pendulum, is swinging back toward a kind of Ur Nil interpretation."[1] This statement returned to my mind in late 1992 when I met John Anthony West in Egypt and we were discussing his work with Robert Schoch on redating the Sphinx. West was responding to criticism from Mark Lehner, who had stated that if there had been a previous civilization that had built the Sphinx, there should be more evidence somewhere of that prior civilization.

West had stated that, indeed, there should be more evidence of other structures buried under the sand than just the Sphinx, and perhaps alternative researchers should trace the course of the ancient Nile to find that information. West never mentioned "another" Nile, but he deserves the credit for stimulating me to pursue that line of thought. When Hakim presented the indigenous traditional view to Bob Vawter in November 1996 that the ancient Khemitian civilization was based on an older river to the west, it was the final key I needed to research and develop this paradigm.

Egyptologists such as Mark Lehner only discuss the geology and history of the current Nile River, and since their paradigms only determine that civilization began in the area around 3100 BC, they do not interest themselves in an ancient river possibly once existing in the Western Desert. But other researchers, such as anthropologist and ecologist Karl Butzer, have done extensive work studying soil deposits and gravels to attempt to trace the early geological history of Northern Africa. There have been varied theories about the possibility of an ancient Nile because of the admitted difficulty in tracing a river's history. The concept of studying a river's layers of deposited alluvial soils may be difficult because the oldest layers have been eroded away. But it is believed that a river roughly corresponding to the Nile had been in existence for millions of years. The argument will be in the exact dating of the features of long since dried up beds and geological rock formations created by the ancient river. According to the work of Butzer and others, evidence in the form of tools and apparent sites of human occupation in the Western Desert dates to over 700,000 years ago.[2] This was a rainy period when a great river (the Ur Nil) existed many miles west of its present course that may have been 300 feet higher and many miles wider than the current Nile. Studies in the geological stratigraphy of soil layers have shown periods of rainfall and periods of arid (desert) conditions in great cycles from 700,000 to 10,000 years ago. The current desert conditions in the Western Desert are less than 10,000 years old.

There is definitely a geological basis to assume the Ur Nil, the western river, was still in existence from 60,000 to 20,000 years ago. In that time span were periods of arid and semi-arid conditions where habitation was difficult but not impossible, and pluvial (rainfall) periods of thousands of years in duration in which the western Nile would have flourished and the Bu Wizzer civilization of indigenous tradition could have existed. Some Egyptologists and geologists assume the western Nile River disappeared well over 100,000 years ago, but geophysical evidence suggests long pluvial periods in the timeframe of 100,000 to 60,000 years ago. This suggests the Ur Nil could still have existed and been the foundation of the ancient Khemitian culture. Hakim had proposed to me after I finished my field work with him in September of 1997 that another trip to Egypt would be necessary to determine if the remnants of the ancient Ur Nil could be found in the four main Oases still existing in the Western Desert. I then agreed that an on-site investigation of those areas was necessary for a complete analysis of the question.

This investigation was undertaken in November of 1998. A team of four people, myself, Abd'El Hakim, Karena Bryan and our driver Mohammed, went on an excursion into the Western Desert and visited the four Oases, known as Bahariya, Farafra, Dakhla and Kharga. It was obvious a much more extensive investigation would be necessary in the future to completely develop the theory of the Ur Nil, but our journey proved to be a very fruitful one.

At the break of dawn we headed south into an intense fog bank. After a few hours we arrived at the Oasis of Bahariya. Located about 120-150 miles south of Giza, Bahariya was an indication of what was to occur on this trip. After hours of typical desert landscape with little vegetation and evidence of any water sources, right outside Bahariya there was suddenly lush vegetation, palm trees and active villages. There was no obvious aboveground water source, and since yearly rainfall is almost nil in the desert, it was clear there was an active, extensive groundwater table that was the source of the water for the vegetation. This key point was present at all the Oases and will be a point for us to return to at the end of this chapter.

We did not stay long at Bahariya, but continued our journey south to Farafra. After another 50-75 miles of barren desert with little signs of life, again suddenly lush vegetation and palm trees appeared on the outskirts of Farafra Oasis. We observed many Egyptians cultivating green fields, and the villages were more than just surviving on these crops. We saw some evidence of older structures with limestone remnants and silt deposits—was this from Bu Wizzer times and the ancient river? This was a possibility, but only speculation at this point. We investigated some mudbrick ruins that Hakim dated to the Ptolemaic dynastic period (ca. 300 BC), so it was certain dynastic Khemitians had been here. Had they built over ancient Khemitian sites? No answers at this point.

We continued our long journey to make it to Dakhla Oasis by nightfall through another 100 or so miles of desert terrain, but it was on this section of the journey that the scenery changed dramatically. Instead of just yellowish sand dunes and miles of emptiness, vistas opened up for us that distinctly reminded me of the American Southwest. Rock formations, mesas, salt and mineral deposits and mountains that appeared straight out of southern Utah and northern Arizona stretched out in the west for hundreds of miles (*see* Figure 62). These geological formations, as in the American Southwest, had to have been formed by great ancient waterways. Geologists recognize that millions of years ago this area of northern Africa was covered by ocean water, and when the ocean receded northwards, the ancient Ur Nil, called the Protonile, Paleonile and Prenile by geologists, moved in from a southern source. The combinations of the ancient ocean and river along with volcanic and seismic activity had carved out the magnificent landscapes we viewed (*see* Figure 63). That there once was an ancient river in the Western Desert seemed a strong

Figure 62.
Western Desert of Egypt. Evidence of some of the
geological formations created by ancient waterways. 1998.
Photo by author.

Figure 63.
Western Desert of Egypt. More evidence of
possible ancient waterways. Near Dakhla
Oasis. 1998. Photo by author.

possibility. The questions remained, when and for how long did it exist?

We made it into Dakhla Oasis under a gorgeous desert full moon. Dakhla was a much larger oasis than Bahariya and Farafra combined, and we observed intensive agriculture with vast cultivated acreage of vegetation and crops, palm trees and obvious extensive ground water sources. Again, there is virtually no rainfall to speak of in the area, and we witnessed no external irrigation, so all was grown by virtue of ground water sources. We spent the night at Dakhla and got up early for more observations. More mudbrick Ptolemaic ruins with evidence of limestone fragments were strewn around the area. Were these limestone fragments the remains of ancient Khemitian structures?

We left Dakhla and made our way southeast for almost another 75-100 miles to Kharga Oasis. Again, once past the outskirts of Dakhla, the landscape changed dramatically. Huge rock formations, marble deposits, buttes and mesas straight out of southern Utah appeared to us and stretched for many miles to the west. We stopped so I could take photographs and we examined what appeared to be an ancient river bed (*see* Figure 64).

At this point an interesting aside occurred. As we paused for me to take photos of the varied formations present, a little duckling came crying out of the desert to us. We were all amazed at this sight as we could not imagine where it could have come from, there being no obvious water sources in the area. It must have fallen off a truck bound for Kharga Oasis as it could not have been living in this desolate area. We rescued the little bird, gave it food and water and brought it with us to the Oasis where we gave it to a young girl to take care of. Hakim pointed out that the duck was the ancient Khemitian symbol for birth, *Sa*, and this was perhaps a confirmation that we had found the birthplace of the Khemitian culture. It was obvious we had given the little duckling a "rebirth" as it could have not lasted much longer in the desert heat and dryness.

Before entering Kharga Oasis, we viewed more incredible formations shaped by the ancient waterways, and we were then greeted again by the now familiar abrupt change to lush greenery and vegetation. Kharga

Figure 64.
Western Desert, facing west. Between Dakhla and
Kharga Oases. Possible evidence of ancient
riverbed. 1998. Photo by author.

Oasis, the largest of the four Oases, featured a large expanse of cultivated acreage with all sorts of grains, fruits and vegetables growing in abundance, again with no evidence of external irrigation techniques except for groundwater pumping and channeling. We investigated the site of a Ptolemaic temple called the Hebis (Ibis) Temple, dedicated to the Neter *Djehuti* (Thoth) whose sacred animal or symbol was the Ibis bird. Hakim maintained this temple was on the site of an ancient Khemitian Per-Ba, and we did find limestone and granite pieces in abundance, evidence of the remains of large monolithic blocks as well as many different styles of potsherds, as we had at all the Bu Wizzer sites.

The next morning at breakfast provided some interesting information. All over Kharga there were signs and billboards advertising the area as "The New Valley." It was obvious the Egyptian government was undertaking a massive development in the area, with high-rise apartment complexes, many construction projects and extensive cultivation of all types of crops. At breakfast we met an Egyptian scientist, a Ph.D. in agronomy, an agricultural expert. He did not speak English and I did not get his name, but Hakim translated the conversation for me. When we discussed the Egyptian advertising campaign for 'The New Valley," he laughed and shared with us his feelings that this area and the Oases were really the Old Valley! When we inquired further into what he meant, he stated quite clearly his belief that an ancient, great river had flowed in this area and the Oases and groundwater were remnants of this great river. We were not able to get a date from him on when the river dried up above ground, but his information was good support for our new paradigms.

We left Kharga Oasis and headed northeast toward the city of Assut. The terrain became even more spectacular on this leg of the journey. We rode up into mountains, several thousand feet up, and here the landscape reminded me somewhat of Colorado, as well as areas of California. We stopped and I was able to take pictures of incredible vistas that extended for hundreds of miles (*see* Figure 65). From the vantage point of several thousand feet up, I could see how the primordial ocean and later Ur Nil river had carved out the valleys and rock formations below. It appeared to me that one could see the full outline of an ancient river bed many miles wide and hundreds of miles long. We could even make out what is known as the Qattara Depression in the north, hundreds of miles away, which is a huge gouge in the earth believed to be the result of the intrusion of the ancient ocean and which may have resulted in a tremendous lake bed. The area was vastly different many thousands of years ago than it is today (*see* Figure 66). Water was abundant, both on the surface and below ground. As the Egyptian agronomist told us, the underground water table has been fairly abundant for millennia, albeit with cyclical fluctuations, and has been a major source of water for humans in this area for hundreds of thousands of years.

When I returned home after the journey to the Oases and Western

Figure 65.
Western Desert, facing west. Between Kharga
Oasis and Assut. Possible site of ancient riverbed.
1998. Photo by author.

Figure 66.
Western Desert, between Kharga Oasis and Assut,
facing east. 1998. Photo by author.

139

Desert, there was much research to do. I spent hours in the University of Colorado at Boulder library delving into the literature about the geology of Egypt and the Western Desert. Of all the books and articles I examined, very few addressed the subject of an ancient river in the west. Those that did refer to the possibility referenced the work of M. L. P Blanckenhorn.[3] As I could not find any of his writings in English (the only references I found were in German and were from the beginning of the twentieth century), I could only study secondary sources about his investigations.

Several works I found confirmed the existence of the extensive groundwater. A report compiled from an international meeting of geologists in Egypt in 1963 provided information about the many observations and investigations by various geologists about the groundwater in the Western Desert. It was stated that there was enough groundwater under the Western Desert of Egypt to supply all of the Middle East with fresh water for many years.[4] This is an indication of how extensive scientists believed the water table was which confirmed our observations in the field.

I believe the groundwater table under the Western Desert to be a flowing river, and not a stationary phenomenon. The water flowing through underground passages gave the ancient Khemitians the idea to drill other passages to link to the natural ones and bring the water to the sites further east. The above ground ancient Ur Nil and underground river were sisters, and as long as rainfall was abundant, fed each other with ample amounts of flowing water. When the climate dramatically changed at the end of the last Ice Age and rainfall severely declined about 10,000 years ago to the present, the Ur Nil dried up, bringing on the onset of the Sahara and Libyan Deserts, and only the underground river has remained.

Hakim had led me to see that the ancient Khemitians had "followed the water" from the west and channeled it to the east. They channeled it all the way to the present Nile Valley, and the water provided the basis for all food and fuel for the ancient Bu Wizzer civilization.

CHAPTER FOURTEEN

ASGAT NEFER—
THE HARMONY OF WATER

IT BECAME APPARENT to me that as a result of our discussions held in California in the summer of 1997, there was a specific focus of research that Hakim was pushing me towards in his elucidation of the Bu Wizzer civilization. He kept emphasizing the primary importance of the role that water played for the ancient Khemitians and kept repeating the particular Khemitian term for water, *Asgat*. He pointed out the prefix *As* was still used in Arabic names, as in Aswan, the beginning of the waters, and Assut, the end of the waters. This seemed to indicate the ancient river flowed only from Aswan to Assut, very short compared to today. However, the modern cities of Assut and Aswan may not be exactly where the ancient river was as the current names could have been borrowed from more ancient sites in different locations.

The emphasis on the importance of water continued in our field work in September of 1997. Creating a picture of underground tunnels for water, above ground aqueducts, channels and huge limestone walls erected for containing water flow, Hakim was emphasizing an ancient civilization totally dependent upon and highly conscious of the uses of the intrinsic properties of water. He continually pointed out a particular glyph, *Asgat Nefer*, and stated his belief that the Per-Neters, Per-Bas and other Khemitian structures were built to utilize the power of water. Asgat, of course, meant water, but it was his specific translation of Nefer that was the key. Nefer has been translated as "beautiful" or "good" by Egyptologists, but Hakim insisted on the translation "Harmony." Harmony in this sense meant beyond polarity consciousness, beyond a concept of good and bad, positive and negative, the state of balance, of non-duality referred to by masters as bliss consciousness. Water, then, contains the essence of Nefer, of being able to maintain and sustain all life forces. The Ankh, long known as the Khemitian symbol for Life and used as the form for keys to open temple doors or gates, also referred to water, in that water was the key to all life.

Of course, most of this sounds obvious to us; we all know we cannot survive for long without fresh water. Science has long known and taught that all life depends on water and may have first evolved in the sea, then moved on to land. Our bodies are mostly water, etc. Yet amazingly, we have taken water for granted for so long that we may have forgotten the most profound qualities and capabilities of water that were known to the ancient Khemitians.

After discovering the glyph Asgat Nefer all over the Bu Wizzer sites (*see* Figures 67 and 68) and seeing the evidence of tunnels, channels, aqueducts, man-made lakes, and the possible existence of the ancient western river as the basis of the previous predynastic civilization, I began to delve deeper into the meaning of water itself. This aspect of the research took me to the work of two men, Viktor Schauberger (1885-1958) and Johann Grander (1930-), both Austrians who were also fascinated by water and the incredible properties it possesses. A deeper exploration of the work and ideas of these two great scientists allowed a far more profound picture to emerge as to the reasons why the Khemitians had engaged in such monumental projects concerned with water.

Many past scientists have involved themselves with research on water, people such as Theodore Schwenk, Fritz Koch, Henri Coanda, Nikola

Figure 67. Sakkara. Temple of Maya. Glyphs on fourth register from left, on bottom, are *Asgat-Nefer*, the Harmony of Water. 1997. Photo by author.

Figure 68. Sakkara. Glyphs in center are *Asgat-Nefer*, the Harmony of Water. 1997. Photo by author.

143

Tesla, Samuel Hahnemann (the father of Homeopathy) and Anton Mesmer. But it also became clear that Schauberger and Grander, giants in this field, stood out from the rest. Both men believed that water is much more than we are taught it is. The two gasses, hydrogen and oxygen, when combined to become the miracle liquid we call water, seem to be designed by a conscious creator to possess and manifest truly divine properties. It seems out of place to bring these concepts into a scientific discussion, using terms such as "divine" and "miraculous" to describe the liquid we all take for granted. But because I have personally experienced both sides of myself, and my science has evolved to be both physical and metaphysical, and because I believe that both Schauberger and Grander perceived these aspects of water themselves, the information in this chapter must be stated this way—water is truly a gift from God and can be the source for all we need in terms of sustenance and energy.

There are several excellent books on the life of Viktor Schauberger, and I will draw on one of the best, *Living Energies* by Callum Coats. I would highly recommend this work for an extended discussion of Schauberger's life and theories, only some of which I will discuss here. Schauberger was born into a family of foresters, people with long histories of observing and working with nature. Viktor shied away from the university education his brothers pursued and spent many years living in isolation deep in the forest, observing nature first hand. Schauberger actually stated towards the end of his life that nature had been his teacher, and this entailed countless hours studying rivers and the dynamics involved with flowing water.

Schauberger observed that the action of flowing water and the subtle temperature variations present in streams and rivers created an incredible complex of energies. He coined the phrase "vorticular dynamics" to describe the swirling, flowing actions of water and its ability to convert potential energy into kinetic energy. Schauberger theorized that in the union of the gases hydrogen and oxygen to produce liquid water, an enormous amount of potential energy was stored in the system. As water flows and increases its vibratory rate, it creates a unique swirling and upwelling pattern that is called Paired Vorticular Dynamics. With this particular flow pattern and dynamic, water produces tremendous amounts of energy.[1] Coats, in his book on Schauberger, mentions the great difficulty in explaining Viktor's complex theories. I, too, have perhaps oversimplified these theories, but I leave the involved technical explanations to those better qualified to do so and for more restricted audiences. It is the general tenor and overall concepts of Schauberger's work that interests and concerns me here.

Viktor Schauberger loved to use the German word *Ur* as often as possible, and he used it to mean "primordial," "original." It was in the same context the term Ur Nil was coined by Blanckenhorn as the original Nile River. Schauberger also viewed the Earth as a living organism and the water flowing through her underground passages as her blood, functioning the same way blood does for our bodies. Not only does water provide the medium and conditions for all the Earth's needed biochemical reactions to maintain life, water provides the energy needed to fuel the whole system. This was the essence, I believe, of Schauberger's work and genius. With the incredible potential of water to produce energy, we have never needed to rely on the burning of fossil fuels or to create the violent, harmful results of nuclear fission and fusion. These activities have led us to the current environmental crisis evident on a global scale and the great disharmony present in our modern systems. Schauberger predicted the current environmental crisis in the 1930s, based on our ignorance of the uses of and abuse in the treatment of our water supplies.[2]

Schauberger discussed two general categories of energy reactions. The actions of the vorticular dynamics of water, reacting internally, he labeled "implosion," and he identified it with the actions of centripetal forces, going inward toward a center point. He called implosion feminine and creative. The action of forcing outwards he labeled "explosion," identified with centrifugal forces, that of flowing away from a center point, and he called explosion masculine and destructive. He observed the dynamics of water being primarily implosive and creative. The major involvement of modern science and technology with explosive reactions for energy production Schauberger observed as masculine, destructive forces out of control and responsible for the imbalances evident in all human endeavor.[3] These sound like extreme value judgments—that anything masculine is destructive, therefore "bad," and anything feminine is creative, therefore "good"—but in nature nothing is wholly good or bad. It is the balance of these forces that is represented by Nefer, the harmony that nature always strives to maintain.

Applying his theories practically, Schauberger developed many inventions and devices that demonstrated his profound knowledge of nature. He totally redesigned the method and techniques of the Austrian logging industry. Up until the early part of the twentieth century, the logging industry had only about a 20 percent yield of logs cut and sent down rivers to the mills. The use of straight pathways and metal flumes were causing the cut logs to be destroyed en mass in route to the mills. Viktor theorized that imitating natural means would produce a more efficient system, increasing the yield. He suggested using wooden (or stone) flumes to imitate the natural flows of rivers and streams in serpentine, undulating formations. At first his ideas were scoffed at, and he was criticized vehemently by the German professors of the science of hydrology. But a few visionary and open-minded professors seeing the beauty of his ideas backed his research. The result was a system that produced better than an 80 percent yield. This system was not given the total acceptance it should have due to the ignorance of those in charge of the industry, stuck as they were in their accepted paradigms.

Many of Schauberger's theories and inventions were appropriated by the Nazi German government of the 1930s and '40s for military application, some of which were the development of jet aircraft and disc-shaped crafts employing implosion technology and anti-gravitics for propulsion. Yes, this is true and may be surprising to many to hear, that the Nazis were testing disc-shaped aircraft in the 1940s which were but a few months from being operational when the war ended. Realizing that water and air were similar mediums, Schauberger also emphasized the natural design of fish bodies who swim on river or ocean bottoms as the ultimate aerodynamic models for airplanes. Witness the design of our Stealth aircraft today, based on Schauberger's theories.[4]

Viktor Schauberger was at odds almost his whole adult life with the academic scientists in the fields of hydrology and physics. Schauberger identified 33 different types of water, none of which are ever mentioned in any current science textbooks. He also maintained the best water for us to drink, optimum for maintaining healthy biological systems, was that which came from the bowels of the Earth, from underground springs and aquifers, full of dissolved carbons and minerals. Schauberger maintained we should never suffer from illnesses such as cancer and heart disease if we continued to drink water from these sources, but instead we devitalize and destroy our water with our modern means of extraction and distribution through straight metal pipes.

Johann Grander, a fellow Austrian, has taken Schauberger's ideas even further. Also eschewing formal university education, Grander withdrew into nature to observe and learn the truth of life's mysteries. Conducting his own experiments with magnetism in order to heal his arthritis, Grander became deeply involved with the use of magnetism for healing. Johann had actually learned the use of magnetism from his father, who had been interested in the varied applications of magnetic energy. This was not a new phenomenon; many scientists in history have been interested in using magnetism and electricity in healing modalities. Sir Francis Bacon, Anton Mesmer, Benjamin Franklin, and others, who were usually associated with Rosicrucian or Masonic philosophies or other schools of mysticism where it has been taught that vibration is the basis of all creation, were pioneers in this type of research.

Grander then began to experiment with sources of power for his inventions of magnetic healing devices and created what he later called a "water battery," using water as the energy source. He discovered that the magnetic energy he created with his machines was transferred to the water itself. By applying electrical and magnetic charges to water, Grander found he could "revitalize" the water by returning it to a pristine energy state. He called his theory "Living Water" and believed he had found the means to cure many diseases.[5] As Schauberger had stated years before, Grander claimed we were destroying ourselves by "killing" our water supplies, using harmful chemicals and metal transport systems which removed the vital essence from the water by severely lowering its vibratory rate. By applying his techniques, he raised the vibratory rate of the water back to its natural, pristine state so it could be used to heal many diseases.

Grander also claimed that water had "memory." Just removing toxic chemicals and bacteria by filtration was not enough; the water still held the memory of the harmful products. Only by returning the water to its natural vibratory rate, by applying electricity and/or magnetism, could the "memory" of those harmful vibrations be removed. Grander has not been alone in the belief that water has memory; both French biologist Jacques Beneviste and renowned German physicist Wolfgang Ludwig, an advisor to the World Research Foundation in Los Angeles, are strong supporters of the thesis.[6] According to Grander's theories, the water we are drinking from municipal sources in our urban centers may be causing people much more harm than good.

A profound understanding derived from the work of both Schauberger and Grander is the knowledge of water's unique ability to lend its vibratory essence to a lesser medium, as well as strip away or remove vibratory essences from a higher medium. In other words, water that comes from deep within the earth, full of dissolved minerals and carbons, will easily give up its essence and nutrients to a human body and invigorate, maintain and restore health. But water that has been denatured, devitalized, carrying the harmful vibrations of toxic chemicals, bacteria and metals, will actually remove nutrients, minerals and vibratory essence from a human body causing great harm and disease. This is why both Grander and Schauberger were so against our modern systems of water extraction and delivery to our urban centers. Not only is our cities' drinking water not providing us with the necessary nutrients we need, but it is stripping our bodies of minerals and necessary chemicals for optimum health and causing great harm to all living systems.

Johann Grander remains a recluse today in Austria and has refused interviews with the media and has rejected invitations to other nations in the West because he has been labeled a "crackpot" by so-called scientists. Viktor Schauberger was abused by both the Nazis in the 1930s and '40s and by American Industrialists when he was coerced to come to the United States in the 1950s. It is to the credit of people like Dr. Walter Schauberger (Viktor's physicist son), Olaf Alexandersson, Callum Coats, Hans Kronberger, Jill Fraser and Dr. Joseph Lancaster that we have any knowledge at all of the work of these two great men.

Research into the work of Schauberger, Grander and others has enabled me to understand the ancient Khemitians depth of knowledge concerning nature and their great wisdom and to realize the direction Hakim has kept pushing me in this research. It was his continued emphasis on the Asgat that brought out the theories now to be presented.

The Rosicrucians and other metaphysical mystery schools teach that all is vibration. What we determine as being physical as opposed to non-physical, organic as opposed to inorganic, are just packets of atoms vibrating at different frequencies. Like frequencies tend to attract each other and resonate in harmony while unlike frequencies tend to cause conflict and disharmony. The frequencies of Nature (also God, if you will) all seek to resonate to some degree of harmony and flow in cycles. The things produced by humans, such as plastics, synthetics, manufactured metals, etc., are all of a lower, different vibratory rate than that of Nature and have tended to upset or cause disharmony in natural systems. This is the essence of our ecological crisis evident worldwide. It has been argued that since human beings are part of nature, everything they make or produce should be "natural" too. But it is obvious this is not so; nylon and dacron do not have the same essence as silk, cotton, linen or hemp. Plastic is certainly not the same as wood or stone, and manufactured metals or synthetic stone do not have the same vibratory essence as natural igneous rocks such as diorite, schist, granite, basalt and alabaster, and sedimentary rocks like limestone.

149

The great Russian Rosicrucian artist and mystic Nicholas Roerich once stated, "When faced with a choice of the Real and the Unreal, always choose the Real." That is to say, with a choice of natural and man-made materials, the natural material will always be better and healthier for the human system. As Schauberger and Grander have taught us, water drawn from the bowels of the Earth will always be better for us in all ways than chemically treated, irradiated water forced through metal pipes.

It has become clear to me that Schauberger and Grander only redis-covered what the ancient Khemitians already knew over 10,000 years ago. When I was discussing the theory of an older Nile River in the Western Desert being the source of the ancient Khemitian's water systems, a geol-ogist named Renee Wilkinson of Boulder, Colorado, put forth the con-tention that what we were looking at was not an ancient river, but only an extensive ground water table that feeds the Oases as that was the source for the underground tunnels. I answer this point by maintaining they were and are the same thing; the above ground Ur Nil and the vast under-ground water were part of the same system, one feeding the other. What seemed obvious in our observations in the field is that the underground water table Ms. Wilkinson is referring to is actively flowing, not standing or stagnant, by virtue of its flowing through natural underground passages that the ancient Khemitians imitated in drilling tunnels to connect to these natural arteries, and is an underground river, the descendant of the ancient Ur Nil. Viktor Schauberger compared the Earth to a living organism, with water being her blood and underground tunnels and pas-sages her vascular system, indicating that water tables are not stagnant normally, but actively flowing to deliver and receive energy and vitality.

My investigations indicate that the Khemitians built above ground aqueducts, and natural stone waterways and channels, and also drilled miles of underground tunnels through limestone bedrock, all for the same reasons—Asgat Nefer, for the Harmony of Water. When both sources were active, the huge above ground Ur Nil, and the vast, extensive under-ground Ur Nil, the water was fully utilized in an elaborate system by the ancient Khemitians as no people have ever done since.

The ancient Khemitians understood the magic of water as the source of life and energy. It is why they chose igneous rocks to be the medium for utilizing the power of water. As mentioned, Christopher Dunn has recently provided us with a powerful theory that exemplifies the Khemitian concept of Per-Neter, the House of Nature. Igneous rocks such as diorite, granite and basalt contain mica, minute pieces of quartz crystal, which will amplify and regulate an electrical current, magnetic field, or any vibratory essence passing through it. Alabaster is African crystal and acts the same way as quartz does. Sedimentary rocks such as limestone contains nummilites, remains of marine organisms, therefore lending an organic essence to the stone, also presenting a different vibratory capability. As Dunn cogently explains in his book, the choice of materials and design for the Great Pyramid was not at the whim of a megalomaniacal king, but scientifically selected by adepts quite aware of the vibrational properties of igneous rock and the science of harmonics.

Christopher Dunn describes the Great Pyramid as acting as a coupled oscillator, a machine vibrating in harmonic resonance with an already vibrating source. That source was the Earth herself, and the Per-Neter was "tuned" purposely to vibrate in harmonic resonance with the Earth, as a seismic tap. Long before I met Christopher Dunn and long before Hakim first met Dunn in 1998, this was exactly the function of the Great Pyramid Hakim first described to me in 1992. As Dunn also points out in his book, another great scientist was aware of these principles, Nikola Tesla, the inventor of alternating current in electricity, a man who had over six hundred patents.

The Per-Neters act as seismic taps, drawing Earth seismic energy, and vibrating in harmonic acoustical resonance with the Earth. This energy can then be utilized for real, practical purposes. What Dunn has brilliantly accomplished in his landmark book is to be able to put the indigenous teachings in modern, technical terms and understanding. This approach has great appeal to all people, particularly engineers and technocrats who are not stuck in the theories and paradigms of Egyptology.

Dunn also explains the internal design of the Great Pyramid in terms of a machine, a power plant, not as a giant mausoleum. Such anomalies as the granite plugs in the ascending passageway, the design of the Grand Gallery and the Antechamber, and the use of only granite in the so-called King's Chamber have never before been adequately explained by Egyptologists, but are accounted for by Christopher Dunn's power plant theory.

The most salient point Dunn makes, for the purposes in this chapter, is his description of the external and internal features of the Great Pyramid in regards to the element of hydrogen. The outer walls of the Per-Neter are "dish shaped" and may have served to collect radio and microwave energy from the cosmos. Dunn tells us the frequency emitted by atomic hydrogen lies in the spectrum of microwave energy—intimating that this knowledge was not only known to the Khemitians, but deliberately incorporated into the design and function of the Great Pyramid. It is here that Dunn makes the point so important that the fuel that was produced by the Giza Power Plant was hydrogen gas.

While I was fascinated with Dunn's ideas when he first shared them with me in early 1997, it was after spending time in the field with Hakim in September 1997 that I became deeply interested. When Dunn shared with me the preliminary drafts of his book in early 1998, all sorts of bells and whistles went off in my head. After delving deeper into the work of Schauberger and Grander and having long discussions with Hakim about Asgat Nefer and the Great Pyramid as a power plant, it all seemed to fall into place as a coherent theory.

In Chapter 11 of his book, Christopher Dunn explains his belief that evidence in the so-called Queen's Chamber of the Great Pyramid indicates that chemicals were used to produce the hydrogen for the fuel of the power plant. According to the indigenous teachings of Abd'El Hakim, the chemicals were not the original source of the hydrogen, but Asgat, water was! With the publication of his book, Dunn provided the scientific basis and engineering expertise to augment the teachings of Hakim, who kept emphasizing to me the primary role water played in the Bu

Wizzer sites.

The ancient Khemitians drilled miles of tunnels through limestone bedrock, created aqueducts and water channels out of limestone, granite and basalt—all to create the phenomenon of running water in a pattern akin to natural waterways, in undulating serpentine pathways which mimic the natural flow of a river, generate magnetic fields and release potential energy into kinetic energy. Water running through igneous rock full of mica caused the stones to vibrate at higher frequencies. Johann Grander stated that running water derives much of its energy from rocks, and in particular, igneous rocks.[7] In a beautiful natural feedback process, the vibrating stones would give energy to the running water, increasing its energy exponentially. In turn, the water would give energy back to the stones causing them to vibrate higher, and so on, ad infinitum, unless disturbed or acted upon by another force.

One of Viktor Schauberger's many great observations was how trout could remain motionless in raging currents. He also saw that the fish were able to swim against the current with very little effort on their part. Schauberger concluded that a certain temperature gradient, that he later recorded to be 4 degrees Celsius (39 degrees Fahrenheit) and which he called "The Anomaly Point of Water," would negate all forces acting upon water and create a perfect homeostasis, a harmony of balance. With no energy surrounding the trout, they could very easily swim upstream as there was no resistance. It was this brilliant observation that enabled Schauberger to invent many great devices utilizing the effects of temperature gradients upon water.[8]

Hakim has continued to point out to me certain features on the Giza Plateau that may illustrate the ancient Khemitian's knowledge of Schauberger's discovery concerning this amazing effect that temperature gradients have upon water. In many spots on the Giza Plateau, one can observe breaks in the limestone pavement stones laid down by the Khemitians. These breaks appear as round or square holes leading to the underground water tunnels (*see* Figures 69 and 70). Hakim states these were for sunlight to enter in and heat the onrushing water. Were the

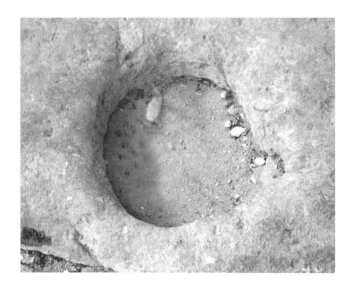

Figure 69.
Giza Plateau.
Round hole in
pavement
stones
possibly for
sunlight to
heat water
underneath.
1999. Photo
by author.

Figure 70.
Giza Plateau.
Square hole
for solar
heating of
underground
water. 1999.
Photo by
author.

Khemitians utilizing natural solar power to heat the water to obtain a certain temperature gradient, an optimum temperature known to the

Khemitians for a specific reaction needed in the Per-Neter?

To continue this hypothesis, the rushing water amplified by the igneous rock heated by solar energy would enter into the Great Pyramid in the underground chamber called the pit. In his scenario Christopher Dunn speculates that chemicals may have been used (anhydrous zinc and dilute hydrochloric acid) to produce the hydrogen for the Giza Power Plant. I maintain the water was broken down by electrolysis or catalytic conversion into its components, oxygen and hydrogen. Dunn goes on to say that the hydrogen gas, greatly amplified and energized by the Great Pyramid acting as a coupled oscillator, could be converted into a source of power for the ancient Khemitians as well as producing radio and microwave energy. Here we have created a paradigm for why the glyph Asgat Nefer appears so frequently at the Bu Wizzer sites. It was the "Harmony of Water" that provided a major source of the energy utilized by the Per-Neters (*see* Figure 71).

I will discuss one last alternative theory concerning the construction methods of and involvement of water in the Great Pyramid. In his book *5/5 2000 Ice: The Ultimate Disaster*, the revised edition published in 1997, author Richard Noone delves into explanations of how he believes the Great Pyramid was constructed. Although I do not agree with his conclusions or explanations, to his credit Noone is one of the few modern researchers to introduce water into the equation of the Great Pyramid. Actually, Noone was quoting the work of a little known inventor named Edward Kunkel, who in the 1930s began to interest himself in the possible ways the incredible tonnage of blocks involved in the Great Pyramid could have been lifted into place. By a process of elimination, he quickly discarded the orthodox theory of extensive physical labor in which blocks were hauled up mudbrick ramps with wooden sledges. Kunkel arrived at the conclusion water was involved in the form of hydraulic pumps to float the blocks into position. Kunkel called his theory "The Pharaoh's Pump" and hypothesized that the Great Pyramid itself was a giant water pump. Noone utilizes Kunkel's theory in explaining how all Khemitian Per-Neters and Per-Bas were built by creating lakes and water pools, and by

Figure 71.
Edfu. Temple of Horus. Glyphs of Per-Neter (pyramid) and Asgat (water) in center. Support for the contention that water was connected to the pyramids as possible energy source. 1999. Photo by author.

raising and lowering blocks of limestone, sandstone and granite into the levels they wanted to place the blocks.

While I applaud the effort of Noone in bringing Kunkel's theories to light and recognizing that the many tunnels and channels on the Giza Plateau were for the delivery of water, I disagree with the chronology and sequence of events. I, of course, contend the tunnels and channels were constructed to bring the water in, as a source of power for the Per-Neter, not for the means of construction. While Kunkel's pump theory is interesting, and according to Noone, Kunkel was awarded a patent for a working model in 1958, I find difficulties in an overall acceptance. Noone inti-

156

mates that water levels would be used to float the blocks to the levels desired. I cannot see, however, how the large blocks of granite, all 43 of them, being nine feet long and weighing an average of 70 tons, could have been floated in this manner and still placed into position so accurately. Noone also describes some sort of chemical engine used in the center, creating a fire to control temperatures, but no residue of chemical burns has ever been found in the area Noone/Kunkel describe. I also find it difficult to imagine water levels floating blocks up to a height of over 400 feet to complete the upper levels of the Per-Neter.

In the original version of his book, Noone postulated a date of 4000 BC for the construction of the Great Pyramid, a date earlier than the orthodox 4th Dynasty date of 2500 BC, but still nowhere near the proposed Bu Wizzer civilization of over 10,000 years ago. I still maintain, in accordance with the indigenous Khemitian tradition, that levitation using acoustical harmonic resonance with igneous rock and water vibrating at ultrasonic frequencies, was used to overcome the force of gravity. Dr. J. O. Kinnaman claimed he and Sir Flinders Petrie found "anti-gravitational machines" and "vibratory devices" in the Great Pyramid that were used in its construction. British Egyptologist Walter Emory found a cache of stone items in a tomb at Sakkara in the 1930s. Among them were many plates made out of volcanic schist with holes in the center. Not knowing what to make of them, he interpreted them as "ceremonial plates for flowers, lotuses." Some of these plates are on display in the Cairo Museum, and I maintain, along with Christopher Dunn, that these plates are parts of machines, perhaps made to spin to produce a sound vibration in order to overcome the force of gravity (*see* Figure 5, page 15). These schist plates may be part of Kinnaman's anti-gravity machines (*see* Figure 72). I have discussed with Christopher Dunn and other engineers the hope for funding in order to produce a working model of the Giza Power Plant and the uses of water to produce hydrogen gas. Some sort of presentation of a practical application of these theories would go far to "justify" these ideas for those who need such proof.

Richard Noone has enthusiastically endorsed the theories of

Christopher Dunn and to his (Noone's) credit has revised his own ideas of the purposes of the Great Pyramid. Noone's introduction of Kunkel's water pump theory has paved the way for the realization of just how important a role water played in the lives of the ancient Khemitians.

It was the harmony of water, the ability of this miraculous liquid, many of whose properties were rediscovered by Schauberger and Grander, that provided the life force and fuel for the whole ancient Khemitian civilization. This also explains why so much effort was expended to build the Per-Neters, to drill so many miles of tunnels, and why this great civilization was able to maintain itself for so many thousands of years before recorded history. I can now also answer the Egyptologists when they ask "where is the evidence," for the evidence is there, in the miles of tunnels with running water inside, in the true meaning of the Per-Neters themselves, and in the artifacts they have uncovered but do not know the uses of. The real question that remains is what happened to end the apparently perfect energy system. Christopher Dunn has also postulated that some great event did occur which ceased the function of the Giza Power Plant—and it is this point that I will address in the next section of this book.

Figure 72.
Cairo Museum. More examples of schist plates.
One in center could have been part of a machine.
1998. Photo by author.

PART THREE:

BRINGING IT ALL BACK HOME

KHEMIT AND THE MYTH OF ATLANTIS

 **W**ITH ALL DUE respect to my favorite poet, Bob Dylan, I will indeed try in this last section to bring it all back home. To bring it all back home entails venturing into subjects not considered by academicians as worthy of a scientific or serious treatment, until the last decade or so. Bringing into this discussion the ideas of the myth of Atlantis or possible extraterrestrial contacts, not only in modern times but also with ancient peoples, will have definite reactions. These "taboo" areas will provide the defenders of academic paradigms just cause to reject, in toto, all the concepts and thoughts presented in this book. But it is not those people with ossified minds and beliefs that I have been addressing myself to from the beginning of this work, but those who can see and feel the glimpses of the coming dawn, where all ideas and subjects will be open for honest and serious discussion.

The topic of the myth of Atlantis has been the focus of varied books and inquiries ever since Plato brought the concept to the Western world in two of his *Dialogues*, *The Timaeus* and *The Critias*, written in the fourth century BC. Plato claimed the story was passed down to the Greek statesman Solon by Egyptian priests. Several other Greek and Roman authors also related similar stories of a great ancient civilization that perished in a series of cataclysmic earth changes. The story of a great flood has been found in the mythology and literature of almost all peoples world-wide, which has convinced many authors that it was a real event. In their book *Cataclysm!*, British science historian D. S. Allan, along with geologist and anthropologist J. B. Delair, present an effective case for the possibility of a world-wide cataclysm occurring very near in time to Plato's dates for the fall of Atlantis around 11,500 years ago.

From my extensive research and interest in metaphysics, I became aware that Plato's Atlantis story, and stories of even older civilizations, such as that of Lemuria in the Pacific Ocean, are accepted parts of the Western metaphysical tradition. Groups such as the Rosicrucians, the Freemasons, the Theosophical Society, the Association of Research and Enlightenment, the Order of the Golden Dawn and the Poor Knights of The Temple of Solomon (the Knights Templar) have all accepted the myth of Atlantis as a real event that occurred in time and space.

In the early 1970s when I first discovered the works of Edgar Cayce and his channelings about Atlantis, I became very interested in the subject and read many books, especially those of Ignatius Donnelly, Robert Stacey-Judd and Manly P. Hall. Cayce's channelings were fascinating and detailed, and based on the accounts of his life story, he seemed to be a very credible source. The linkage of Atlantis to ancient Egypt was also particularly strong in Cayce's channelings, and for a while it seemed logical to me in my research in its early stages in the 1970s that Egypt had arisen as a result of a migration of advanced beings from the doomed Atlantic island continent. It is also somewhat interesting that Mark Lehner, so often mentioned in this book as one of the strongest proponents of the accepted paradigms of academic Egyptology and highly doubtful of the existence of any previous Khemitian civilization before the dynastic periods, started his career as a follower of the channelings of Edgar Cayce and wrote a book in 1974 in which he supported the story of Atlantis and an ancient Khemitian prehistory.[1]

In 1979 when I first heard the tape of the lecture given by Dr. J. O. Kinnaman, it was his declaration that he and Sir Flinders Petrie had found "proof" of Atlantis with ancient records and anti-gravitational machines in the Great Pyramid that so fueled my interest in his life and work. It was Kinnaman's declarations that were the final "key" for me, that obviously Atlantis had been a reality. It seemed early in the twentieth century, before Cayce had even channeled any information linking Egypt and Atlantis, that Kinnaman and Petrie had found the physical proof! Of course, it could be argued quite the opposite since Kinnaman did not discuss this information in public or private before the 1950s and Petrie apparently never publicly discussed any such alleged finds, that Kinnaman only made the story up after the publication of Cayce's readings in book form. This argument has been presented to me often by skeptics of Kinnaman's claims, and quite frankly, it cannot be refuted at this time. Since I have stated that Kinnaman claimed he and Petrie entered into an agreement with the governments of Egypt and Great Britain never to divulge the finds in their lifetimes, it remains speculation.

However, there was another claim of Kinnaman's that has recently, due to the work of Christopher Dunn, appeared to have some justification. Kinnaman stated that one of the uses of the Great Pyramid was to serve as a giant radio station to send messages all over the earth. Kinnaman claimed there was a passageway off of the secret entrance they found on the south-east corner of the Great Pyramid that led to a spiral staircase that took them down over 1,000 feet into the limestone bedrock. There, in a large room lying on a stone table, was a giant quartz crystal ground convex that was 30 feet in every direction (long, high, thick etc.). This giant crystal with thousands of prisms inserted in it was the source of the radio transmission.

One of the researchers who has been very supportive of the possibility of previous high civilizations existing over 10,000 years ago has been David Hatcher Childress. A prolific writer and world traveler, Childress has authored several books about lost cities around the world. In his book *Lost Cities of North and Central America*, Childress mentions finding an article in a 1960s edition of *Arizona Highways* magazine which revealed that Egyptian artifacts had supposedly been found in the Grand Canyon in 1909, and the story had been written up in the *Phoenix Gazette* newspaper. Childress set out to investigate and found copies of the newspaper articles in a public library. Sure enough, the story was front page news in the *Phoenix Gazette* for two days running in April of 1909. These front page articles discussed the discovery of a cave in the Grand Canyon in Arizona containing Egyptian mummies and artifacts. The find was supervised by a Professor S. A. Jordan of the Smithsonian Institute, but when Childress called the Smithsonian to attempt to verify the discovery, the head archaeologist and other officials of the Smithsonian denied knowing about any such excavation or artifacts. In fact, the Smithsonian archaeologist stated categorically that no Egyptian artifacts had ever been found in North America, and there never had been an S. A. Jordan who was associated with the Smithsonian.[2] In the Denver Museum, I was able to locate back copies of the Smithsonian's annual reports. I did not find the year 1909, but in the 1911 report, the name S. A. Jordan was listed as a field archaeologist for the Smithsonian Institute.

In a discussion I had with Dr. A. J. McDonald, President and Executive Director of the Kinnaman Foundation in 1994 about Childress' revelations of an Egyptian find in the Grand Canyon, Dr. McDonald related to me that one of the places Kinnaman had stated radio messages from the Great Pyramid were sent was to the Grand Canyon in America. Now, again it is possible as an informed archaeologist Kinnaman may have known about the Grand Canyon find in 1909, and even known Professor S. A. Jordan, and just connected the discovery to the Great Pyramid, but it remains an interesting story nonetheless.

We also now have Christopher Dunn stating that by virtue of the Great Pyramid acting as a coupled oscillator, tremendous amounts of microwave and radio wave energy were produced. So, indeed, the Great Pyramid could have functioned as a giant radio station, just as Kinnaman said it did. Hakim has stated on many occasions that the indigenous tradition has taught that one of the many functions of the Great Pyramid was as a giant communication device—again linking our three sources together in a new paradigm of the Great Per-Neter.

Now I can also weave other disparate pieces of information together into a coherent tapestry. In 1992, I engaged in a series of protracted discussions with Hakim on the subject of Atlantis. At that time he presented a very dim personal view of the myth of Atlantis, a pose which quite frankly greatly surprised me. He stated there was no real "proof" of the myth and Plato may have fabricated the story of Solon receiving the information from Egyptian priests. When I brought up Edgar Cayce and the Western mystery school traditions of Atlantis, Hakim stated that they all were just following Plato's lead. The motivation Hakim expressed for taking this stance was the way the Atlantis myth was used, to indicate that "Non-African people created the monuments" (i.e., the Pyramids, Sphinx, etc.). Hakim objected to the possibly racist way the myth of Atlantis had been utilized, namely, "an enlightened group of white people" escaping a dying continent and civilization came to Africa and taught "ignorant, backward indigenous peoples the trappings of civilization." I should mention that it was clear that Hakim was expressing his opinion of the way the myth had been utilized to promote a racist sense that Africans were not capable of creating high civilization without a Caucasian boost. I have mentioned that Hakim is a vigorous Afrocentrist, and his opinion of the Atlantis myth reflected that stance. Hakim adamantly adhered to his belief in the indigenous Khemitian tradition that Khemit was an advanced civilization and the cradle of humanity, and did not need "Atlanteans" nor anyone else to teach them how to build pyramids and other stone structures.

As one who had been deeply immersed in the Rosicrucian and Western mystery school tradition for many years, I was disturbed by Hakim's stance. I pondered over our conversations for many years without broaching the subject again with him. However, after Hakim's public emergence as an indigenous Khemitian wisdom keeper and master, I brought the subject up again in 1997. At that point, I posited a variation on the theme. As we had already engaged in lengthy discussions of

163

ancient Khemit and the Bu Wizzer sites, I proposed to him that the myth of Atlantis was a mythologue, that is, a general story passed down that referred to the Global Maritime Culture that existed before the "flood," before the cataclysm of 11,500 years ago, a civilization that was centered in Northern Africa, in ancient Khemit. I further proposed that if there indeed was a continent of Atlantis in the Atlantic Ocean off the coast of Africa, it was connected to Khemit, both by trade and tribal bloodlines, and not in any way a separate, more advanced civilization. Hakim was pleased with the postulation and had no problem with an "Atlantis theory" if ancient Khemit was a major part of the equation. This theory sits very well with me, too, as I now believe the Atlantis story relayed by Plato (who was an Initiate of Khemitian mystery schools and the indigenous tradition) was indeed referring to Khemit by utilizing the theme of Egyptian priests relating the story to Solon, and there were other reasons for his version. One of those reasons may have been that Plato, as an initiate of the Khemitian tradition himself, was bound by oath not to divulge the whole story and to protect those still keeping the tradition alive in the dynastic Khemit of his day.

I now also believe Dr. J. O. Kinnaman may have been using the general Atlantis myth in the same way. Perhaps having found evidence of the ancient Khemitian civilization, he then equated that evidence with the known myth of "Atlantis," also connecting it all with the Masonic tradition he was a part of. In other writings, Kinnaman had indicated he knew that ancient Khemit was much older than orthodox Egyptologists believed.[3] In presenting this story to a group of Masons, Kinnaman may have used the myth of Atlantis as a catch phrase, as Plato had done, because he knew the time was not ripe for the indigenous Khemitian tradition to be revealed (even to Masons!).

Now, Christopher Dunn has brought more information into this tapestry of Atlantis. Dunn discusses in his book the reliefs that are found in the underground crypts at the Temple of Hathor in Dendara of Upper (south) Egypt, reliefs that indicate the Khemitians were perhaps aware of the principles of electricity (*see* Figure 73). The Temple of Hathor at

Dendara where these reliefs appear is a relatively late dynastic temple, dating from the Ptolemaic Period, ca. 100 BC. In one particular panel of the reliefs in the lower crypts, a baboon is shown holding two knives up in front of the apparent giant light bulbs (Crookes tube), perhaps deflecting the flow of electrons (*see* Figure 74). Many authors have attempted to interpret these reliefs, such as Joseph Jochmans and Moira Timms, but none has had complete access to the indigenous tradition. Hakim states that what is shown on these reliefs was not knowledge of electricity known to the dynastic Khemitian priests who had them carved, but a previous understanding of energy known to the ancient Khemitians long before the dynastic periods. He further stated that the baboon, a companion symbol of *Djehuti*, Thoth, the Neter of wisdom, was holding the knives as a warning. What was being shown was a knowledge of energy known to and utilized by the ancient Khemitians that could be, and had been, abused and misused.

Hakim's explanation of the Dendara reliefs leads us to return to Christopher Dunn's observations inside the Great Pyramid. It has also led to a coalescence of what Dunn stated in his book and what I have proposed in the previous chapter. As mentioned, Dunn has stated he has seen evidence that chemicals were used to produce the hydrogen generated by the Giza Power Plant. Dunn bases his theory on several observations: the first being salt encrustations deposited around the southern shaft on the south wall of the so-called Queen's Chamber, which he believes was the place where the chemicals were mixed and the reaction occurred, thereby leaving the salt as residue of the reaction. He also states that the presence of the two shafts entering into the chamber were not for the conveyance of a dead king's soul (as believed by Egyptologists and even alternative theorists), but for the conveyance of the two chemical solutions, proposed by Dunn as possibly being an anhydrous zinc solution and dilute hydrochloric acid. The resulting reaction would produce hydrogen gas and zinc chloride precipitating out as a salt, thus explaining the salt encrustation on the walls of the Queen's Chamber. Dunn also mentions the dark-stained walls of the northern shaft of the chamber,

Figure 73.
Dendara.
Temple of
Hathor.
Reliefs in
lower crypts
of temple
possibly
showing
knowledge of
electricity by
depicting
ancient
Crookes
tubes. 1999.
Photo by
author.

Figure 74.
Dendara.
Temple of
Hathor. Relief
in lower crypt
showing Isdes
(baboon,
companion of
Thoth) holding
knives in front
of possible
Crookes tube.
1999. Photo
by author.

166

possibly where the acid was deployed and reacted with the limestone walls, indicating two different chemical solutions were used and why two shafts were created (*see* Figure 75).

Dunn then proposes an "accident" occurred, an explosion in the King's Chamber that virtually ended the utilization of the Great Pyramid as a power plant. In his theory, the chemical reaction took place in the Queen's Chamber and the hydrogen gas was then delivered to the King's Chamber, which resonated in acoustical harmonic resonance with the hydrogen, greatly amplifying and intensifying it. But one day the reaction got out of control, and a great explosion occurred, ending the process. Evidence for the explosion mentioned by Dunn is the bulging out of the granite walls of the chamber and cracks in the granite beams in the ceiling (*see* Figure 76). Egyptologists have explained the cracks in the granite as the result of an ancient earthquake, but as Dunn points out, the evidence for earthquake damage is not consistent. There is no evidence of earthquake damage in the Descending Passage leading to the subter-

Figure 75.
Great Pyramid of Giza. Northern shaft in Queen's chamber showing dark stains on limestone walls. Support for Chris Dunn's theory that acid may have been used to produce hydrogen gas in Great Pyramid. 1998. Photo by author.

Figure 76.
Great Pyramid. Cracks in granite ceiling of King's Chamber. Egyptian Government has since repaired these cracks. 1992. Photo by author.

ranean chambers, which goes into the limestone bedrock and which would be much closer to the epicenter of an earthquake and should show much more damage than that of the King's Chamber much higher up in the internal structure of the pyramid.

Upon reviewing Dunn's preliminary manuscript (at his request) prior to publication in 1998, I must admit his theory presented some problems. Already having decided, from the influence and insistence of Hakim, that water, Asgat, was the source of the hydrogen and energy of the Great Pyramid, I was greatly impressed with Dunn's logic and observations and had to reconcile these apparently divergent theories. My own personal observations in the Great Pyramid in 1997 and 1998 had led me to agree with Dunn that an accident had indeed occurred in the King's Chamber. The walls of the chamber do obviously bulge out and can be seen to be separating from the floor. I have taken photographs of the ceiling cracks, and no one else but Christopher Dunn has attempted to explain the discoloration of the granite stone box (erroneously referred to as a "sarcophagus") in the chamber. Cut from Aswan rose granite, the box today is a chocolate brown, not the natural color of the granite. Dunn proposes the discoloration is from the accident, a great explosion that caused a chemical reaction in the granite, greatly darkening its color.

Now I can weave this tapestry together and present a hypothesis tying in the last chapter and what I have stated so far in this one. I propose, synthesizing the works of Viktor Schauberger, Johann Grander, Christopher Dunn, and the indigenous teachings of Abd'El Hakim, that indeed water was the original medium and source of energy of the Giza Power Plant. When the Per-Neter was originally completed as a functioning power plant, in my opinion well over 20,000 years ago (Kinnaman had stated he and Petrie found "proof" the pyramid was over 36,000 years old), water was the source of the power, catalytically converted to oxygen and hydrogen in a beautifully controlled implosion reaction.

In our lengthy discussions on the subject, Christopher Dunn had proposed a dilemma for me. If water was the original source for the hydrogen gas used by the Giza Power Plant, then why were there two shafts in the Queen's chamber, the reaction chamber, when only one would be necessary if water was the medium used. The answer came to me after long hours of meditation and thought on the subject. Browsing through my many books with scenes of the temple reliefs, my eyes stopped on one scene which provided the answer. A familiar scene on many Per-Ba (temple) walls depicts the "king" as the realized initiate, being anointed with water by two of the Neters, Djehuti (Thoth) and Horus. I have called this scene "The Two Waters" and have seen it over and over again since the initial revelation (see Figure 77). In the spirit of Schauberger's elucidation of many different types of water, it has become obvious to me the Khemitians also recognized different waters and were depicting two specific ones in these scenes. Djehuti, although depicted as a male Neter, is a Lunar, feminine principle, wisdom (wisdom is also feminine in the Tibetan tradition). Horus is a Solar Neter, a masculine principle (perhaps that of compassion, as in the Tibetan tradition). It now became clear to me why Hakim had spent so much time showing us two different tunnel systems, one deep underground and the other closer to the surface. The reason for two shafts to deliver the water into the Queen's chamber is that two types of water were utilized—a cold water coming from the underground Nile, through the tunnels under the Giza Plateau, lunar in nature, feminine, and a heated water coursing closer to the surface through basalt and granite and charged with solar power, masculine in energy, coming through the round and square holes cut into the bedrock for that purpose.

This, then, is the meaning of Asgat Nefer in practical usage by the ancient Khemitians. Using both feminine and masculine waters com-

Figure 77.
Kom Ombo. Temple of Sobek-Horus. "The Two Waters," depicting king anointed with water by lunar principle, Thoth (left), and solar principle, Horus. 1999. Photo by author.

bined provided a Nefer state to produce tremendous amounts of hydrogen in a clean, implosion reaction. This reaction went on for many thousands of years, with a seemingly endless supply of power by virtue of the great pluvials, rainy periods, to produce the water needed for the hydrogen. But something happened; perhaps great periods of drought occurred due to radically decreased rainfall, and the Ur Nil dried up or was radically decreased, resulting in a depletion of the water source. Another possibility is that consciousness declined due to the waning of the senses as the Age of Aten (The Wiser) came to a close and water was abandoned as the source and chemicals substituted, or a combination of both. Whatever the reason, the use of chemicals led to the staining and salt precipitation Dunn mentions, and instead of the creative implosion reaction (as per Viktor Schauberger and Johann Grander) of the wondrous Asgat Nefer, a destructive explosion occurred, as stated by Christopher Dunn.

Therefore, the crypts of Dendara may be telling this exact story of a misuse of a great energy known to the ancient Khemitians and warning of a possible future occurrence. I propose this explosion, this "accident," in the King's Chamber may have occurred between 12,000-6,000 years ago and is a real event that was incorporated into the myth of Atlantis. A problem that does arise with this explanation, and which has been voiced to me in presentations I have given over the last few years, is how could the ancient Khemitians, being in advanced states of awareness and consciousness, have resorted to the use of chemicals and allowed this accident to occur. Further complications with this idea are that the 12,000-6,000 year timeframe would be in the Khemitian age of Aten, the time of full use of the senses and flowering of consciousness. I do admit that this is still a problem for me today, but the fact remains that the crypts of Dendara present a warning of the misuse of knowledge and technology and an accident did occur in the Great Pyramid. With the drying up of their water source, the Ur Nil, the waning of the senses as Aten moved closer to the time of Amen, and the world cataclysmic event occurring around 9500 BC, a collective fear could have forced the ancient Khemitians to resort to the use of chemicals and an explosion reaction for their source of energy and power. As Edgar Cayce stated in his readings, Atlantis fell as the result of a misuse of its power and technology, and a disregard for natural law. The reliefs at Dendara warn about a past misuse of energy, the "Fall of Atlantis." I propose the myth of Atlantis was given to the Greeks as a metaphor for real events that happened in ancient Khemit, and indeed, Khemit and Atlantis were not separate civilizations.

Further explorations into the Khemit-Atlantis connection occurred in 1999. As mentioned in the beginning of this book, I have been for many years interested in the work of George Gurdjieff. A series of articles written by William Patrick Patterson for *Telos* Magazine entitled "Gurdjieff in Egypt" and a subsequent video released by Patterson with the same title rekindled my interest in Gurdjieff's work. In his second book, *Meetings With Remarkable Men*, Gurdjieff had stated that he once had seen a map of "pre-sand Egypt" in the possession of an Armenian monk. This map had stimulated Gurdjieff to go to Egypt and search for teachings about human origins in ancient wisdom schools.[4]

Patterson had also been fascinated with Gurdjieff's travels to Egypt and had done extensive investigations of his work. Patterson is convinced that Gurdjieff had seen an image of the Sphinx on the map of "pre-sand Egypt" and went to Egypt to investigate for himself. Of course, I contend that if the map was indeed of a "pre-sand Egypt," it would have contained the pyramids as well as the Sphinx at ancient Giza before the current desert conditions. According to Patterson, Gurdjieff had stated that his teachings had come from a complete system of "Esoteric Christianity" that originated in ancient Egypt many thousands of years before the time of Jesus. I met Patterson at a talk he gave in Denver, Colorado in July of 1999. Both Patterson and I agreed that Gurdjieff might have come in contact with the indigenous tradition over 100 years ago, especially in his extended stay in Ethiopia. Gurdjieff adamantly maintained that the source of all modern esoteric systems had their origins in predynastic Egypt, essentially supporting our paradigms of ancient Khemit.

However, Patterson also mentioned other statements of Gurdjieff that stimulated further investigations on my part. Gurdjieff had stated in his writings and discussions that he had found inscriptions on the walls of the Temple of Horus in Edfu, which is in the south of Egypt, that mentioned the myth of Atlantis. In his articles Patterson mentioned a book by British Egyptologist E. A. Reymond, *The Origins of the Egyptian Temple*, in which translations of the texts of Edfu were given. Reymond called these inscriptions "The Building Texts" and claimed they were the myths of the origins of ancient temple buildings.[5]

I found Reymond's translations of the Edfu texts to be incoherent and poorly done and decided to discuss these texts with Abd'El Hakim in Egypt. On our tour in October of 1999, we went to the Temple of Horus at Edfu and found the inscriptions on the walls ourselves. It became apparent to us that the texts at Edfu were copies of much older texts, the temple having been built in the Ptolemaic period ca. 200 BC, and were discussing events that had taken place in ancient Khemit many thousands of years before the temple was built. Gurdjieff had stated that the texts spoke of an advanced people, whom Reymond referred to by the standard Orthodox translation of the term Neter, as "Gods" who had come from an island that had been destroyed by a flood and had brought their wisdom to the ancient Khemitians. However, Hakim's interpretation was vastly different. I believe the texts are referring to the time of the ancient Ur Nil over 30,000 years ago when the vastness of the river had turned all of Northern Africa into a series of large islands. As the Khemitians became united, they moved from island to island, erecting temples and pyramids and creating the ancient Khemitian civilization. Once again, this became a basis for the future myth of Atlantis. Hakim was definite that the texts were not referring to a more advanced non-Khemitian people coming from outside Africa and teaching the Khemitians how to build in stone. I propose that the ancient people followed the river from the south and the west and formed the union of the 42 tribes in the Land of Osiris, Bu Wizzer, and other ancient sites in the south, such as Edfu and Abydos. The texts are therefore describing the Khemitian's ascension into higher consciousness, becoming "one" with the Neters, opening their senses and creating high civilization. The texts discuss how the "Neters arrived" from different islands and began the process of erecting large-scale edifices in stone. We did not find any references to cataclysms, but even so, the ancient Khemitians may have "island hopped" until the 42 tribes united and coalesced into a coherent civilization.

There may have been an advanced island civilization in the Atlantic (or Antarctica, as has been claimed) that perished as a result of the great cataclysm proposed around 11,500 years ago. But it may also be that there were large islands in Northern Africa as a result of the ancient Ur Nil around this same time that were populated by an advanced civilization of ancient Khemitians. The Myth of Atlantis may have referred to the entire Global Maritime Culture that existed in many parts of the world prior to 10,000 years ago, much of which was almost completely destroyed by cataclysmic events. I believe ancient Khemit should be included in that mythology.

Ancient Khemitian priests may have entertained Greek travelers with stories of cataclysms destroying island civilization as an oral history of the Global Maritime Culture that once existed, knowing full well that ancient Khemit was part of that past glory, but not revealing the complete story to the "barbarian" Greeks.

CHAPTER SIXTEEN

THE EXTRATERRESTRIAL QUESTION

THE TOPIC OF ATLANTIS is enough to make most academics cringe and turn the other way, but when I bring the subject of extraterrestrial contact into the mix, some so-called scientists get ready to throw stones. The subject, however, has fascinated people since the modern wave of sightings began in 1947, over 53 years ago! I have also been deeply drawn to this subject ever since I had my first sighting around the age of eight in the early 1950s. Growing up in a six-floor apartment building in the Bronx, New York, I used to like to go up on the roof at dusk, still one of my favorite times of day. One late August afternoon, I was on the roof, lost in my thoughts, when I spotted three lights in the sky in formation, going from northeast to southeast towards Manhattan. When the lights reached about due south, they made a 180-degree turn and headed back to the north, then totally blinked out. I remember quite clearly thinking, even with an eight-year-old mind, that those were not ordinary airplanes. I never spoke of this incident to anyone until 1986 when I was interviewed for a book concerning my research with crystal skulls.

This incident fueled my deep interest in UFOs and the science "fiction" movies of the 1950s. It is beyond the scope of this book to document the whole "movement" since 1947, but my interest in possible contact with ancient human civilizations by beings from other worlds began in earnest in the early 1970s. It was a little known book, *Mankind-Child of the Stars* by Max Flindt and Otto Binder, published in 1974, but based on work written by Flindt as early as 1962, that stimulated me to take seriously the possibility that humanity did not evolve on this planet but was the result of genetic engineering by other beings. Many others whose works are better known, such as Erich Von Daniken, Zecharia Sitchin, Arthur Horn, William Bramley, Neil Freer, Bruce Rux, and Lloyd Pye, have written on this subject, but to my knowledge Flindt and Binder were some of the first researchers to posit this hypothesis.

Flindt and Binder's work was much more scientifically documented and oriented than the more popular Von Daniken (who has been soundly criticized for poor scholarship), but I read all of Von Daniken's works and was impressed with the many archaeological anomalies he presented. However, it has to be the prolific writing and scholarship of Zecharia Sitchin that has had the most influence on me and others investigating this subject. Sitchin started his journey into what he has termed The Earth Chronicles with his first book *The Twelfth Planet*, published in 1976.

I did not discover Sitchin's work until the early 1980s, but once having done so, read his books fervently ever since. Although there are some disagreements I have with his theories concerning ancient Khemit, his general theme of another planet in our solar system, called by the ancient Sumerians *Nibiru*, which had an advanced civilization that had been involved in the creation and evolution of human beings, continues to interest me greatly. Sitchin's translations of Sumerian cuneiform texts, some only in fragments over 5,000 years old, are vastly different than those of other Sumerian academic scholars. Sitchin translates the texts quite literally when they discuss the gods flying around in crafts and interacting with human beings.

Of course, most anthropologists and biologists have totally rejected Sitchin's theories, but over the last 25 years Sitchin has spawned many "children" and champions, such as Drunvalo Melchizedek, Neil Freer and Lloyd Pye. In his book *Everything You Know is Wrong*, Pye presents an effective argument that Darwinian evolutionary theories can explain neither the origins of life nor the origins of humanity. Pye concludes that only the theory of extraterrestrial intervention can completely account for all the "jump starts" evolution would have had to undergo to produce the species we call Homo Sapiens Sapiens—us!

Although I support the distinct possibility of genetic manipulation by other, advanced beings in creating humanity, I have not been convinced by Sitchin, Pye and others that it was one group, the Annunaki of Nibiru, who were the only ones making contact with ancient people. In my delving deeper in the indigenous Khemitian traditions and other literature in the UFO field, a much bigger picture began to emerge.

Over the past seven years Hakim has taken a somewhat nebulous stance on the subject of extraterrestrial life and UFOs. On the one hand, he has been very skeptical of many sightings and abduction stories, believing they are meant to spread fear in order to control people, a position he will not support. On the other hand, he has presented evidence to me that indicates he certainly believes the ancient Khemitians had contact, and that the existence of life on other planets and in other dimensions is a distinct reality and part of the indigenous tradition of the Khemitian wisdom keepers. What is clear to me is that he has presented information that indicates he supports much in Sitchin's theories, but the Annunaki were by no means the only group that had contact with the ancient Khemitians.

In support of Sitchin, Hakim has pointed out to me the distinctly Mesopotamian style of architecture present at the courtyard complex at Sakkara. This would indicate that there was an ancient Sumer long before academicians have recognized a Sumerian civilization, well over 10,000 years ago. It is possible that the Annunaki may have had an influence at Sakkara in its original creation by the Khemitians. Hakim has also related a piece of information that may not even be known to Zecharia Sitchin, that there is a small town on the Mediterranean Sea in Northern Egypt in the Delta Region that has the name *Nibiru*. Hakim states the people of Nibiru have been known as exceptional fisher people for many thousands of years, and when they cry out in the markets in all places in Egypt, "fish from Nibiru," all the people rush to buy their wares. The fact that an Egyptian town should have a Sumerian name, a name that was used for another planet in our solar system, could indicate a connection between the Annunaki of Nibiru and ancient Khemit.

My differences with Sitchin arise when he attempts to credit all of Khemitian achievements, i.e., the pyramids, etc., to only the Annunaki of Nibiru and sees all the Neteru (Gods) as being the actual Annunaki. My research indicates many groups may have had contact with the ancient Khemitians, and one major group came from the star system of Sirius. Robert Temple and Murry Hope have both written books documenting the Khemitian's great interest in Sirius. It was Temple in his book *The Sirius Mystery* who related how the African tribe called the Dogon had vast knowledge of Sirius being a binary star system long before modern astronomers discovered a companion star to Sirius just in the twentieth century, now called Sirius A and B. It is possible, and quite probable, that the modern Dogon are the descendants of one of the original tribes of Khemit, and this is where their information came from.

As Murry Hope points out in her book *Ancient Egypt: The Sirius Connection*, the ancient Khemitians had an advanced and accurate calendar based on the heliacal rising of Sirius. The dynastic Khemitians linked that heliacal rising (around July 23rd - 26th) to the annual flooding of the Nile, an event on which so much of their crops depended for survival. Many of the Khemitian myths linked the Neters to Sirius, especially Ptah, Sekhmet, Isis and Osiris (Wizzer). In fact, a conversation I had with Hakim in the Cairo Museum in 1997 greatly intensified this connection for us. I told him that I had for years been trying to find a meaning for the Khemitian word for Sirius, written by the Egyptologists as *Sopdet* (Sp.dt). Hakim said the Egyptologists had written the word wrong; it should have been S.pth, which he said was *Sa-Ptah*, The Birthplace of Ptah. When he said this, Robert Vawter and I looked at each other and our jaws dropped to the floor. Were the Khemitians saying directly that Ptah was from the Sirius star system?

Furthermore, Hakim informed me that Ptah was referred to as "He Who Comes from the Blue" and was always depicted with a blue head

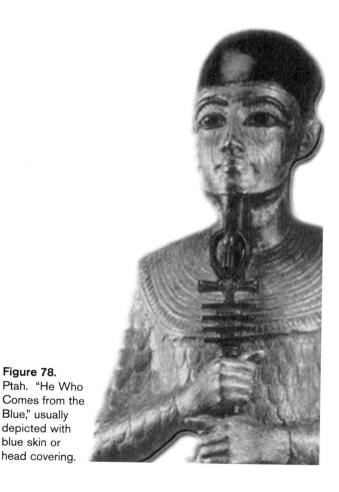

Figure 78.
Ptah. "He Who Comes from the Blue," usually depicted with blue skin or head covering.

covering or with blue skin (*see* Figure 78). Hakim has challenged me to test and chemically analyze samples we have collected in the field of the blue pigment the Khemitians used in their wall paintings, beads and pottery as he maintains it is not cobalt or lapis lazuli, and as far as I know, the pigment has never been completely identified.[1] Was he indicating that the blue pigment, related to Ptah as "He Who Comes from the Blue," may not have a terrestrial source? Was the pigment from Sirius as was Ptah? These are all questions that may be answered once I can do spectrographic analysis of the samples I have collected, tests I hope can be funded and conducted in the coming years. Hakim also told me to study reliefs and statues of Ptah in order to determine what race he represented. Ptah is usually depicted with Asian eyes, a Caucasian nose and Negroid lips. He apparently represents many races as the "Father" or progenitor race from Sirius. Ptah became known as Dyas or Zeus to the Greeks and later "pater" (father) to the Romans: Ptah, Pater, "Father-Race." In 1999, Hakim further elaborated on the translation of Ptah, as "The One Who Comes from the Blue, through the Waters, from the Stars." Clearly, he was indicating the Khemitian indigenous tradition for Sirius as a "star seed" hypothesis for human origins.

The female consort of Ptah was *Sekhmet*, one of the many Lioness-headed Neters of the Khemitians. Her name literally means "The Power," as the term *Hemet* meant "Woman of Power" (incorrectly translated by Egyptologists as "Wife," but no such concept existed in ancient Khemit). Sekhmet's face is often still found on walls of Per-Bas with the blue pigment intact, connecting her also with Sirius (*see* Figure 79). Other Lioness Neters such as Tefnut, Men-Het and Mut have also been identified with the Sphinx, being itself half lion, half woman. Robert Temple has identified the Sphinx with Anubis, or *Ab-Nub* in Khemitian, the Jackal-headed Neter, and therefore also with Sirius, as Sirius is known as the Dog Star. But to quote Karena Bryan, we do not necessarily know "the ancients connected the dots the same way we do," meaning the Khemitians may not have seen Sirius as a dog, as the Greeks did. We know the Khemitians identified Sirius strongly with Isis (Wizzet, Auset),

Figure 79.
Kom Ombo. Temple of Sobek-Horus. Sekhmet, blue pigment still evident on her face linking her with Ptah (left) and Sirius. 1999. Photo by Theresa L. Crater.

sister-consort of Osiris (Wizzer), as part of both dynastic mythology and the indigenous tradition of ancient Khemit.

The Sphinx-Lion-Sirius connection also has an interesting aspect with two other books written by Murry Hope. Ms. Hope channeled the information in these books, entitled *The Lion People* and *The Paschats and The Crystal People*. Many people react negatively to channeled information, as in the Cayce readings, as they oftentimes cannot be verified or documented. I learned early in my mystical training not to reject any source of information out of hand. When I worked professionally as a staff research scientist for the Rosicrucian Order, AMORC, I tested, under strict scientific conditions, so-called psychics, who we preferred to call sensitives. I learned from experience to treat our intuitive aspects seriously. The beings Murry Hope channeled in those two books call themselves the *Paschats*, from the name of a cat-headed Khemitian Neter called Pasht and the French word for cat, chat. They claimed to be leonine beings, bipedal (walking upright like us) who have evolved into the fifth dimension and are currently no longer in dense third dimensional bodies like ourselves.

The Paschats claimed to be very much connected to the ancient Khemitian culture; therefore, the many leonine Neters depicted by the Khemitians could represent them. Hakim strongly identifies the Sphinx with Tefnut, a lioness Neter whose name means "Spittle of Nut," as she was the first physical manifestation of the Sky Neter, Nut. Tefnut is one of the oldest Khemitian Neters, and like Sekhmet, was strongly connected to Sirius according to the indigenous tradition. Therefore, I propose that the Sphinx, said by the indigenous tradition to be over 50,000 years old, relates to Sirius and the Paschats, not to the constellation of Leo as has been postulated by Robert Bauval and Graham Hancock and, therefore, dated by them to around 10,000 BC, at the last astrological period of the Age of Leo.[2] I believe the Sphinx faces a particular heliacal rising of Sirius in the east, not the rising sun according to orthodox Egyptology. I exchanged correspondence with Murry Hope in 1992 and shared with her my ideas of the Sphinx being connected to Sirius and the Paschats, and she enthusiastically agreed (*see* Figure 80, color insert).

The strongest support Abd'El Hakim has given for possible contact between the ancient Khemitians and extraterrestrial beings concerns the Bu Wizzer site of Abu Ghurob. Hakim has always maintained to us that Abu Ghurob is a very old site, perhaps one of the oldest, if not the oldest, occupation site in all of Khemitian prehistory. As we mentioned, all throughout dynastic time periods Khemitians journeyed to Abu Ghurob to make offerings at the great alabaster Hotep, the offering place to the Neters. I have speculated that the alabaster structures, called basins by Egyptologists, were certainly not used for animal sacrifice. Hakim has suggested that the structures may have had some connections to machines and/or were used by "aliens" for the landings and take-offs of their crafts.

The indigenous tradition speaks of Abu Ghurob as an ancient landing site, and that is how we refer to it. A landing site for whom has never been clearly stated. I realize this is all highly speculative, with no real "proof," no indisputable evidence of an extraterrestrial presence, but it does fit in with the "Star People" stories many indigenous elders are now relating all over the world.

Many authors in the last few years have connected Khemitian mythology with that of the star system of Orion. This trend has been popularized by engineer Robert Bauval, who in 1994 presented this idea along with Adrian Gilbert in their book *The Orion Mystery*. Bauval further developed this theory in the book *The Message of the Sphinx*, co-written with Graham Hancock and published in 1996. However, the connection of Khemitian mythology with Orion is by no means original with Bauval, having been also proposed by Jane B. Sellers in her book *The Death of Gods in Ancient Egypt* and even earlier by anthropologist Alexander Badawy and astronomer Virginia Trimble. Bauval uses these authors in his books, so he has given proper credit, but he is usually cited as the prime proponent of this theory. Bauval believes the Giza Pyramids are laid out according to the stars in the Belt of Orion, and other pyramids relate to other stars in the Orion constellation. Researcher Larry Hunter has extended Bauval's theory and believes he has identified the sites that correspond to the other stars in the Orion group. However, the indigenous teachings do not support the emphasis on Orion that these researchers state. Badawy, Trimble, Sellers, Bauval, Hancock, and Hunter all point to the so-called "Pyramid Texts" as the foundation for their Orion theories.

These texts have been dated at the end of the 5th Dynasty of the Old Kingdom Period (according to accepted chronology), around 2350 BC. I believe these texts have been mistranslated and their importance greatly overemphasized by orthodox Egyptologists and the alternative researchers mentioned. Appearing first in the so-called Pyramid of Wenis (not Unas), the texts are magical spells, supposedly to protect a dead king's soul. Bauval et al. interpret the texts as a magical rite of passage, identifying a dead king's soul with Wizzer (Osiris), and then connecting Wizzer with the star system of Orion. The term mentioned by Bauval, *Sahu*, supposedly connects Wizzer with Orion. Jane Sellers in particular has forwarded this belief, stating, "In one of his aspects he (Wizzer) was called Sahu. Through work on ancient Egyptian sky calendars, this is widely acknowledged to correspond to our constellation ORION."[3] Again she states, "Translators do indeed consistently translate the name Orion for the Egyptian Sahu."[4] Many researchers have taken off on these points, therefore believing Orion to be the source of the Khemitian mysteries, the origin of Wizzer/Osiris. However, in a conversation I had with Hakim in October of 1999, he denied that the term Sahu has anything to do with Orion. Hakim translates Sahu as, "The One who knows but keeps silent," indicating a connection with the wisdom of Wizzer but not in any way related to the Orion star system.[5]

For years I have questioned whether the Pyramid Texts were the pure, unadulterated mystery texts many researchers have claimed. Now Abd'El Hakim's voice and indigenous knowledge has been added in differing with this opinion. Hakim cites the late date of the texts (2350 BC), while he also cites the tradition of the written record (the Suf) of the Khemitians going back 6-8,000 years ago. All researchers agree the texts appear to be copies of earlier texts, but none of the "original" texts have been found. Certainly no such texts have been found in any of the so-called 4th Dynasty pyramids, but it is assumed the same process, that of identifying the dead king with Wizzer and therefore with Orion, existed all throughout the Old Kingdom Period.

I reject the concept of Sahu as identifying Wizzer with Orion. The traditional Khemitian teaching has been to identify Wizzer with Sa-Ptah (Sirius) as with the other Neters, Isis, Ptah, etc. On our tour in October of 1999, I had the great opportunity to visit the Temple of Osiris at Abydos in the south of Egypt with Hakim for the first time. Described by orthodox Egyptologists as a temple built by a king with the name of *Seti I*, they proposed that it was constructed around 1250 BC. Hakim maintains there was no one "named" Seti, that this was a title held by many kings. The Per-Ba (temple) is also much older than the 1250 BC date assigned to it and is a sacred, ancient Per-Ba dedicated to Wizzer. The Per-Ba, containing wonderful reliefs with the original paint still in evidence, is also one of the best preserved in all of Egyptian archaeology. One of the great teachings that I have learned from Hakim is to be able to differentiate styles of the reliefs as to their age. Almost without exception (although there are a few), raised reliefs are older than incised reliefs. Raised relief speaks for itself; the scene and symbols are raised up from the surface of the stone, while incised reliefs are chiseled into the stone.

Figure 81.
Abydos. Temple of Osiris. Examples of raised reliefs. Glyph for Isis is in the center. 1999. Photo by author.

The reliefs at the Temple of Abydos are beautiful examples of ancient, raised reliefs, much older than the 1250 BC date assigned to them (*see* Figure 81). Abydos was an ancient site dedicated to Wizzer and the Per-Ba was erected to the Neter, not to any one king. The reliefs of Wizzer at Abydos show him with blue skin—not green or black as mentioned by other authors, but blue skin (*see* Figure 82, color insert). Clearly, this is identifying Wizzer with Ptah and Sirius, not Orion. Hakim dates the Temple at Abydos as being thousands of years earlier than the so-called "Pyramid Texts" in the Pyramid of Wenis at Sakkara.

A short distance from the Temple of Osiris at Abydos is an even older Per-Ba known as the Osireion. Also dedicated to Wizzer, this structure, only in ruins, is some 50 feet lower than the aforementioned temple, but amazingly is dated to the same time period by Egyptologists. One does not need to have a Ph.D in archaeology to logically assume if a structure is located some 50 feet or more lower than another structure, without any naturally raised hills or cliffs present, then the lower structure must be from an earlier archeological layer and therefore be older than the first, but this logic seems to have escaped most Egyptologists. The Osireion, very reminiscent of the structures in front of the Sphinx at Giza, is composed of huge, megalithic blocks of granite (*see* Figure 83). The dynastic Khemitians, whom Egyptologists believe built this temple, mostly used the softer stone, sandstone, to construct their Per-Bas, not granite as did the ancient Khemitians. In fact, Hakim dates the Osireion as being over 50,000 years old, being near the timeframe of the Sphinx and her related structures. There are a few scattered inscriptions at the Osireion, but they are incised dynastic markings, made many thousands of years after the structure had been built. Also at the Osireion is a symbol made popular by the work of Drunvalo Melchizedek, the Flower Of Life. However, this symbol was made with red paint and does not appear to be an original mark (*see* Figure 84). Hakim dates the symbol anywhere from 300 BC to AD 300, and I believe it may have been made by followers of the schools of the great Greek mathematician, Pythagoras, as he and many of his followers were initiated into the Khemitian wisdom teachings of

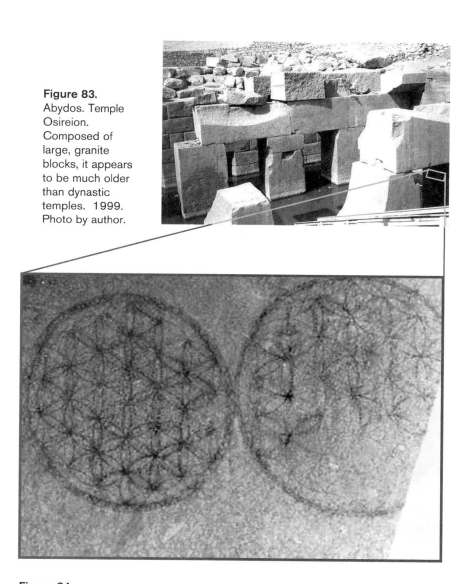

Figure 83.
Abydos. Temple Osireion. Composed of large, granite blocks, it appears to be much older than dynastic temples. 1999. Photo by author.

Figure 84.
Abydos. Temple Osireion. Flower of Life symbol on wall. 1999. Photo by author.

sacred geometry. It certainly could have been that the ancient Per-Ba, called the Osireion, became a teaching temple of sacred geometry, and many Greeks (who are erroneously credited with "inventing" geometry by academicians), such as Pythagoras, Thales, Euclid and Plato, could have been initiated there.

In respect to his Orion theory, another concept that Robert Bauval and others use is that of *Tep Zepi*, translated by them as the "First Time." This term is referred to as Tep Zepi in Bauval's first book, then *Zep Tepi* in his second book on the subject with Graham Hancock. Bauval sees this term relating to the time of Wizzer and, connecting this to his Orion theory, places the date around 10,000 BC. But Hakim adamantly states there was no "First Time" to the Khemitians, as they did not conceive of a beginning or an end of creation. Existence is understood as a myriad of cycles, with the commencement of the current cycle occurring over 65,000 years ago. The time of Wizzer was thought of as an ancient era not related to any movement of the star system of Orion, and possibly connected to the start of the present cycle, Kheper, the dawn, certainly greater than 10,000 years ago. In William Patrick Patterson's articles concerning George Gurdjieff's trip to Egypt, he stated that the term "Zep Tepi" was mentioned by British Egyptologist E. A. Reymond as having come from the walls of the Temple of Horus at Edfu.

I mentioned in the last chapter that I was able to obtain a copy of the book *The Origins of the Egyptian Temple* for myself. Reymond cited the term *ntr ntri hpr m sp tpy* as the full expression that Bauval has mentioned, and Reymond translated it as "The Sanctified God who came into being at the First Occasion." Reymond puts it in the context of a creation myth, of a time when the Neters first manifested to humans.[6] I discussed this idea with Hakim, and we examined the texts on the temple walls. Once again, Hakim did not believe the texts were discussing a time of original creation, but the time when the Sesh, the people, had achieved a level of consciousness, the flowering of the senses in the current Khemitian cycle, begun over 65,000 years ago. I believe this time period was between 20-60,000 years ago when the Khemitians had attained the consciousness to build their great structures, drill the tunnels for water, and create their civilization, which formed the basis of the later creation mythology. The time period of 12,000 years ago would have been in the stage of Aten in the Khemitian chronology, the full flowering of the senses (and the waning of the Ur Nil), not a beginning as stated by Bauval et al., and not connected to cycles of the Orion star system.

Another interesting concept came into play in regards to the texts on the walls of the Temple at Edfu. Mentioned first by R. A. Schwaller de Lubicz and later by John Anthony West, Robert Bauval, Graham Hancock, Zecharia Sitchin, Barbara Hand Clow and many others, is the term *Shemsu Hor*. Translated by Schwaller as the "Followers of Horus," it is believed by most authors mentioned that they were an advanced people who entered Khemit in prehistorical times and brought knowledge and civilization with them. Zecharia Sitchin believes they were extraterrestrials, in essence the descendants of the Annunaki. However, the translations of E. A. Reymond do not use the term "Shemsu Hor," but the terms *Seshu Hor* or the *Sebtiu*.[7] The first term is translated as the "People of Horus," but it may have a very different connotation than the definition used by Schwaller et al. Again, I engaged in detailed conversations on these points with Hakim in October of 1999 at the site of the Edfu texts. Hakim maintains his stance that there was not an "outside" people, neither Atlanteans, extraterrestrials nor anyone called the "Followers of Horus" who came from outside Khemit and taught the people advanced knowledge in the current Khemitian cycle. The indigenous tradition is very clear that the Sesh came into full consciousness on their own, according to preordained cosmic cycles.

However, Hakim did have an interesting take on the term Seshsu Hor. Instead of interpreting Hor as others have done, that of identifying with the dynastic concept of Horus as the king or with an introduced kingship through the myth of Isis-Osiris-Horus, Hakim relies on the indigenous translation of Hor or Horus as the realized human male. Before a concept of kingship evolved in Khemit in the early dynastic time period, perhaps ca. 4000-3000 BC, Hor was used as the term for the male who had achieved a flowering of the senses, a degree of enlightenment. It had nothing, originally, to do with royalty, but later became the basis for the male chosen by the female as her consort (she as Hat-hor) in the matrilineal descent patterns prevalent in ancient Khemit. What I believe the texts at Edfu are referring to with the terms Sep Tepi and Seshu Hor is the time period in the current Khemitian cycle when men, the male, came into a high state of consciousness and used all their senses (the Neters) and began large scale building in stone and created the Bu Wizzer civilization.

I return here to a discussion of the Pyramid Texts. These "prayers," which should rightly be called funerary psalms as these structures were not true Per-Neters, but Per-Kas, were the trappings of a religion created in the midst of this dynastic period of the Old Kingdom and a deliberate distortion of the true Khemitian wisdom tradition. The rising importance of the priesthood, called the *Hanuti* in the Khemitian language, and the increasing desire by them to control information and access to the inner mysteries, stimulated them to create a religion around the mythos of Wizzer. Using the symbol of the king as the High Initiate, the Enlightened One, in reality the one with the wealth and means to sustain the Hanuti in their new-found status of power and greed, the priests then identified the king with the wisdom of Wizzer, as Sahu.

Instead of revealing the knowledge of Wizzer, Ptah and the Neters as aspects of consciousness, as a means for the people to reach enlightenment, or even as past vistors from the Sirius star system, the truth of these principles was restricted to only the priesthood. The priests then became the spokesmen for the Neters, and only they and the royal families (and they only with the permission of the priests) had access to them. The original knowledge of the Neters and their connection to Sa-Ptah (Sirius) was obfuscated, and if Orion was mentioned in the texts (which may be debatable), it was substituted for Sirius by the priests to create a false religion and to keep the inner mysteries to themselves. The timeframe for this was the Age of Amen, 4-6,000 years ago, the rise of Patriarchy. By substituting the role of the male king as being all important instead of the true Per-Aa, the matrilineal High House, the Hanuti began the distortion of the Khemitian teachings in keeping the knowledge hidden from the Sesh, the people. Does this not seem like the template that led to the creation of all future religions from that time forward?

I do not mean here to belittle or diminish the fine work of researchers such as Robert Bauval, Graham Hancock and Jane Sellers. The paradigm of archaeoastronomy is a valid one, and I believe there are indeed star connections to Khemitian sites. Orion is not a major one, according to Abd'El Hakim, and I would urge those on this path of research to look seriously into the connections to Sirius, as well as the Pleiades and others. Again, I reiterate the indigenous Khemitian teaching that there were originally 42 tribes that made up the Khemitian civilization. Could this also mean 42 different directions in the sky, 42 different star seed lineages? These could include the constellation of Lyra with the star Vega, Sirius, the Pleiades, Arcturus, Aldeberon, Andromeda, Alpha Draconis, Auriga, the Reticulum System, as well as Orion and Nibiru. All of these star systems may have had, and still have, active planets with advanced life forms that have been channeled to individuals or mentioned in the UFO literature as having possible contact with humans past and present.

In discussions I have had with Barbara Hand Clow over the past few years, she has stated that what Christopher Dunn and I are doing is bringing in a new third dimensional paradigm for the purpose of the Great Pyramid. She maintains that there is a higher validity to the work of Jane Sellers and Robert Bauval, that there are indeed higher dimensional star connections to the Great Pyramid and other Khemitian structures. I certainly agree with this contention, and the Orion star system may play a role in this. After all, we do agree the Great Pyramid had many functions, that of the Per-Neter to be an energy device being a primary one, but not the only purpose. The indigenous tradition in the person of Abd'El Hakim states the Great Pyramid was also used for communication, in agreement with Dr. J. O. Kinnaman's declarations that the structure also served as a giant radio station. Barbara and I have agreed the communications may have been on different levels, all around the

Earth in a third dimensional sense and to other star systems in a multi-dimensional sense.

A further teaching of the indigenous tradition that disagrees with Bauval's lining up the three major Per-Neters at Giza and the stars of the Belt of Orion is that there may have been more than three Per-Neters originally at the Bu Wizzer time of ancient Giza. Hakim has spoken to us of another Per-Neter south of the small pyramid called Menkaura, which may have been completely quarried to where little remains, and even another one further south still hidden under the sands. Another project for us to undertake would be major investigations of the area south of the Menkaura Per-Neter to see if there is any evidence of other pyramids having been there.

I believe all the Bu Wizzer Per-Neters formed what has been called a Fibonacci Spiral, and that is the reason they are on a curved, not straight line (*see* Figure 85). Drunvalo Melchizedek, in his book *The Ancient Secret of the Flower of Life*, has presented this idea as relating to the Giza Pyramids.[8] In a private discussion I had with Drunvalo at the Prophets Conference in Phoenix, Arizona in October 1997, I discussed this idea of the pyramids and the Fibonacci Spiral. Drunvalo has taught that energy goes into the Earth near Giza and exits from the Earth near Hawaii, and this is confirmed also by the indigenous Khemitian tradition. Hakim has consistently maintained that near Giza is where energy flows into the Earth. I proposed to Drunvalo in 1998 that we had located the center of the Fibonacci Spiral at Zawiyet el Aryan where the mosque is but that we could not access because of fundamentalist Muslims. He was very interested in this information and that the word "Zawiyet" meant angle in Arabic. Is it the "angle" of the Fibonacci Spiral that is being referred to? Could this be such a powerful spot that the knowledge of its energy is still known and protected by the current controllers of the site, Islamic leaders? This sounds like a similar case to the Dome of the Rock in Jerusalem, sacred both to Judaism and Islam.

I was privileged to hear the late Hopi wisdom keeper Thomas Banyanca speak in Denver, Colorado, in November 1996. Besides dis-

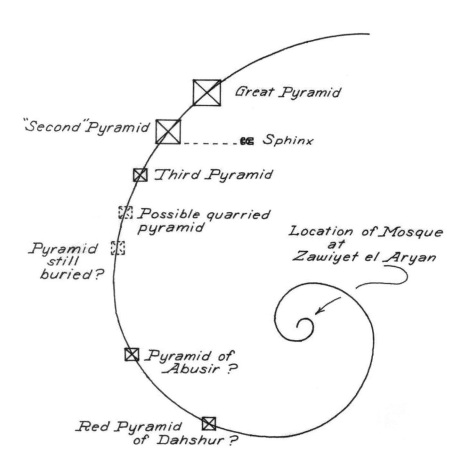

FIBONACCI SPIRAL of BU-WIZZER

Figure 85.
Depiction of Bu Wizzer *Per-Neters* (pyramids) on a
proposed Fibonacci Spiral. Drawing by Paul E.
Bowman, 1999.

cussing Hopi prophesies of near future possibilities for humanity, he also spoke about Hopi beliefs that they were the "original people" and their stories of their ancestors coming from the stars. Lakota medicine man Standing Elk has produced a series of conferences in the late 1990s known as the Star Visions Gatherings. In these conferences elders from many Native American tribes have shared their traditional stories of their ancestors' connections to different star systems. In a *Denver Post* article of January 2, 2000, written by Patricia Gonzales and Roberto Rodriguez, there is mention of Mayan Daykeeper Hunbatz Men lecturing about the ancient Maya traveling all around the world in 2700 BC. In the same article the authors mention Mayan elder Don Alejandro, of whom we have spoken before, lecturing to a North American audience and speaking of the Naga Maya, the ancient Maya who came from the Pleiades. I add to these indigenous teachings the tradition of the ancient Khemitians, that beings from many different star systems visited ancient Khemit hundreds of thousands of years ago. These traditions have been passed down in oral teachings amongst indigenous wisdom keepers all around the world for thousands of years. Serious researchers can no longer deny or ignore these indigenous traditions, and it is time for people of the West to listen to and hear these stories with open minds and hearts.

CONCLUSIONS

THE SUBTITLE OF THIS book is "An Introduction to Khemitology," and, indeed, an introduction is all I intend. I would urge everyone reading this book to also read *Egypt and the Awakening*, co-authored by Abd'El Hakim Awyan and Karena Bryan, for a more expansive exposition of the indigenous Khemitian teachings. The primary goal here was to first establish a framework in order to discard the outdated and inadequate paradigms of academic Egyptology and then present the beginnings of a new discipline, to ferment the revolution Professor Thomas Kuhn had labeled a "paradigm shift" back in the 1950s. But entrenched ideas and fossilized thinking do not give way easily, and the writing of this book has been the easy part.

The long hours in the field, the review of sites already excavated, the analysis of data already interpreted according to accepted paradigms, the countless hours of reading and reviewing the many theories presented, and the thousands and thousands of hours spent in debate and discussion spanning over 30 years of serious research with many disparate individuals and their varied opinions and biases—this has been the easy part, relatively easy at any rate because it all was a tremendous labor of love, with the burning catalytic overriding impetus that the whole truth was not being presented.

Every image I looked at, whether it was the Sphinx, the Great Pyramid, the temples, the statuary, the reliefs, the inscriptions, the pottery, the jewelry, the papyrus scrolls, all the remnants of the culture and civilization that has been called ancient Egypt, ignited a fire within me that could not be cooled, a thirst that could not be quenched, a desire to know that could not be satisfied by Judeo-Christian-Islamic texts, by Greco-Roman texts and by modern academic scholarship. Only through delving deeply into the Western and Eastern metaphysical traditions was a way opened, and that way led to a house in the modern Egyptian village of Nazlet el Samman in Giza, Egypt.

The meeting with the Remarkable Man, the indigenous master of the ancient Khemitian tradition, Abd'El Hakim Awyan, has been the food for my soul. The inner knowledge that those people who created that marvelous civilization had to have been in touch with, and connected to, the source of all that is—much more so than what had ever been taught before—is now fully realized in the living embodiment of Khemitian wisdom within the man Abd'El Hakim. In the coalescence of indigenous teachings now crystallized by elders, women and men all over the planet, Hakim brings forth this wisdom for the prophesized coming of the new dawn of consciousness.

The 4-6,000 year cycle of Imen/Amen, The Hidden, is now coming to an end. All over the world people are awakening, as if from a long dream, to demand answers that religions, universities, governments and those others who have controlled the flow of information have not provided. According to teachers such as Drunvalo Melchizedek and Barbara Hand Clow, this time of awakening appears to have been encoded in our DNA, as if this is all God's plan from the beginning.

I certainly do not believe that I have all the answers and that I am right and everyone else is wrong. All the enlightened masters who have ever walked this plane have all taught the same thing, that Enlightenment cannot be passed from one person to another, and that each individual must find their own truth within as well as without. But masters are way signs, providing road maps of time tested and honored ways to realize the "big picture," to reconnect to the Source.

Abd'El Hakim Awyan presents an indigenous tradition from a long ago people, the ancient Khemitians, who were truly enlightened, in direct communion with the 360 Neters, the "Principles of Divine Creation," possessing complete circular consciousness, as Karena Bryan terms it. That there was, and is, divine creation is a realization profoundly obvious to me, and it is a continual process. That is why there could not be a Zep Tepi, a First Time, just as the first Hebrew word of the Torah, The Old Testament, *Bereshees*, poorly translated by the Greeks as *Genesis*, and mis-understood in English as "In the Beginning," could only refer to a new cycle, never an actual beginning. The Khemitians taught there was no beginning or end, only the cycles in the middle, and this knowledge is now being echoed in the fields of theoretical and quantum physics.

Even the opinions, theories, ideas and paradigms expressed here are only those for this moment in time and space, and may undergo serious revision by a further spark of light to come tomorrow. Although he is a superb archaeologist, prehistorian and historian, Abd'El Hakim does not concern himself with the past or future, only the eternal now. This, of course, presents a paradox, as he speaks of past cycles and the coming new dawn of consciousness. But in essence it is not, as awakening to one's full potential and consciousness means to live in the eternal now where the past and future merge.

So this introduction to Khemitology has presented the seeds of new paradigms based on teachings so ancient they predate our Western civi-lization by tens of thousands of years. These teachings were from a peo-ple so spiritually aware that they were able to create a sophisticated tech-nology, not antagonistic to nature and natural law, but in total harmony with it. This technology enabled them to cut through granite and basalt as if they were butter, to carve and mold these substances with a modern space-age precision and artistic beauty that cannot be duplicated today, to handle weights from 200 tons and more, much more, as if they weighed nothing at all. These things cannot, and will never, be explained with just a limited understanding of who we are and where we have come from.

Most researchers point to the blocks in the Great Pyramid and in the structures in front of the Sphinx to indicate the size of the huge blocks that had to be quarried, dressed and moved into their present positions. Egyptologist Mark Lehner appeared on a Nova Public Broadcasting television special and believed he demonstrated how the dynastic Khemitians could have built a pyramid by hauling blocks of limestone with ropes on wooden sledges. Never mind that the largest block he used weighed only one ton and they had to bring in a front-end loader to complete the task, he actually believed he proved his point. But lying in the Aswan quarry, over 500 miles to the south of Giza where all the rose quartz granite was quarried for the Khemitian Per-Neters and Per-Bas, is an unfinished granite obelisk estimated to be 110 feet long and weigh approximately 1180 tons! The obelisk was unfinished, not because the ancient (not dynastic!) Khemitians could not move it, but because a crack was discovered in it, after it had been cut and dressed (*see* Figure 86).

I should state here that in our disagreements with prominent Egyptologists such as Mark Lehner and Zahi Hawass, I also do not mean to ever make these disagreements personal. For too long, in written works and on the Internet, not only were there major disagreements between Bauval, Hancock, West et al. and Zahi Hawass, but also a series of back-biting, name-calling incidents, hardly worthy of all concerned. This has finally ceased, with an apparent "reproachment" reached between all parties. While some other researchers have questioned the motives of Bauval et al. in this new-found arrangement, it certainly is better for all of us than was the case before. Obviously, I disagree with almost all the theories of Lehner and Hawass, but do not disrespect both men or their academic colleagues. Both men, in particular Dr. Hawass, but also Dr. Lehner, have done much to increase interest in Egyptology and the Giza Plateau. Dr. Zahi Hawass was actually responsible for preventing Robert Vawter and myself from being victims of extortion in 1997 and was very cordial to

Figure 86.
Aswan. Unfinished granite obelisk lying in quarry.
Estimated to be over 100 feet long and weigh
almost 1,200 tons! 1998. Photo by author.

me, and showed the utmost respect for Abd'El Hakim.

The ancient Khemitians had no problems with tremendous weights and huge sizes of blocks because gravity was not a limiting factor to them.

199

They looked to what the Neters had provided for them to create their civilization, all the marvelous things abundant on this great planet. They used igneous rocks, granite, basalt, diorite and alabaster, full of mica, quartz crystals, able to vibrate and resonate with the Earth herself, and full of the material essential for the creation, maintenance and sustenance of life—water. Few people realize that the majority of water found on our planet is not in the oceans, rivers and lakes but rather bound up in the igneous rocks of the Earth.

I am overjoyed to discover daily the many researchers delving into the mysteries of water and writing books about their discoveries. One man, Malidoma Patrice Somé, who is an indigenous African wisdom keeper, has written several books illuminating the great spiritual teaching about water that comes from the heart of Africa. He states, "Water resets a system gone dry in which motion is accelerated beyond what we can bear. African healing wisdom looks at physical illness as a fire moving a person's energy beyond the limit of what he or she can bear. This suggests that we all need water, and need rituals of water, to stay balanced, oriented, and reconciled."[1]

Somé seems to be talking about the concept of Asgat Nefer as taught by Abd'El Hakim, and we can visualize that the ancient Khemitians engaged in spiritual ritualistic practices at the Per-Bas with the water, as well as using the liquid as a physical energy source in the Per-Neters.

The miraculous nature of water, rediscovered by Viktor Schauberger and Johann Grander, was well understood and utilized by the Khemitians. Using the most abundant element in the known universe, hydrogen, for the fuel to power their civilization, and water as the source for that fuel, is a clear indication of their profound knowledge and wisdom.

The 42 tribes came together in a collective awareness, not as Jews, Christians, Muslims, Hindus, Blacks, Whites, Browns, Yellows and Reds, but as the Sesh, the people. Where did they come from? In their myths of Wizzer (the "Good King"), of Ptah (He Who Comes from the Blue), of Hathor (The House of Hor), of Nut (the Sky)—they were all said to be children of the stars. Drunvalo Melchizedek has said, "God uses people to create people."

Are all the mythological beings simply our extraterrestrial ancestors who came down and genetically engineered the human race and taught the Khemitians and all ancient peoples the sacred knowledge of our true origins? Or do they symbolically represent forces from subtle dimensions interacting with the third dimensional levels of being? Perhaps it is not an either/or situation, and both preceding statements are equally true of the actuality of the full experience on this magnificent planet Earth.

These are all questions that deserve to be treated and researched seriously. I fervently hope this book will stimulate some minds, particularly young ones, to look into all these areas with fresh insights. I have presented some seeds; may they fall on the ground and flourish.

I have stated often in presentations that "There are no extraterrestrials, in that we are them, and they are us." I also state that we are the descendants of the ancient Khemitians, and that we have the inherent potential to create magnificent Per-Neters and Per-Bas. Baghwan Shri Rajneesh, known also as Osho, once stated we are all enlightened; we just have to wake up from our sleep and realize it. George Gurdjieff taught exactly the same thing, that we are asleep and need to awaken to our enormous potential.

Our explorations have laid down a framework for this new awakening. I realize this is just a beginning; much more fieldwork needs to be done. I have seen the remnants of the great ancient river, the Ur Nil, in the Western Desert of Egypt and in the modern oases (*see* Figure 87, color insert). It is apparent there is a geological and climatological background to provide a basis for our new paradigms. A period of abundant rainfall existed in Northern Africa about 50,000 to 30,000 years ago, called by geologists the Mousterian Subpluvial. In this rainy period the ancient western Nile could have been actively flowing and provided the means to allow for the emergence of the present cycle of the Khemitian civilization. An unstable phase of rainfall and drought conditions from 30,000 to 15,000 years ago could have stimulated the Khemitians to

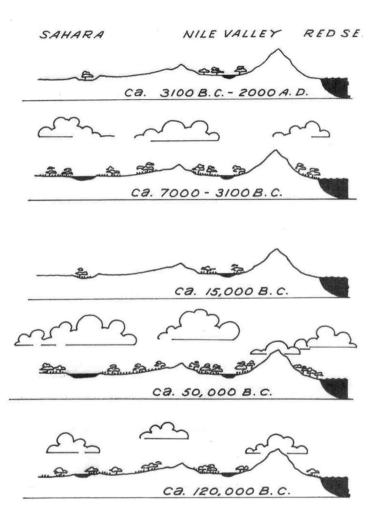

Figure 88.
Diagram showing climate changes in northern
Africa and existence of Ur Nile in western desert
area. Based on information found in Michael
Hoffman, *Egypt Before the Pharaohs*. Drawing
created by Paul E. Bowman, 1999.

migrate eastward and enabled them to return to the Bu Wizzer sites (which were already at that point recognized as ancient sacred sites from previous cycles). With the great climactic and geophysical changes around 15,000 to 12,000 years ago, the great western river dried out, the desert conditions began to dominate the landscape, and the current Nile began its heyday (*see* Figure 88). The Khemitian civilization paused but did not end and emerged again around 8,000 to 6,000 years ago.

We are now at the point of beginning to be able to realize our past greatness. At an area in Sakkara, one can go to the ruins of a sacred Per-Ba. There are three windows constructed out of the limestone, left, right and in the center. If you put your head in the first, you feel joy, warmth and positive energy. When you put your head in the second, you feel dread, cold and fear. But when you put your head in the center window, you feel bliss and oneness. This is the demonstration of Nefer—Harmony. The Khemitians lived in Nefer and understood the ways and means to go beyond polarity consciousness.

They demonstrated this awareness by their use of water—Asgat Nefer. On a fellucca ride on the Nile at Aswan, Hakim told me the Nubian people, particularly the Matokke tribe, still speak the closest modern tongue to the ancient Khemitian language. Hakim implored me to ask our captain, a young Nubian man, to say in his own language, "to go get water." At first he did not understand my request, but when I persisted, he replied, "asbani asagatta!" Khemit still lives in Egypt and can be awakened in all of us.

It is with the concept of Asgat Nefer that I will end this discourse. Viktor Schauberger early in the twentieth century and Johann Grander in the last 40 years have maintained that we have to save our water if we intend to survive as a species. Schauberger provided the theoretical basis, and Grander has provided the practical devices to re-energize and revitalize our water into "Living Water." If the ancient Khemitians have left us one profound bit of wisdom to raise our consciousness in preparation for the great shift, the New Kheper (dawn) phase, it is that we must save our water supplies.

So we raise our glasses (of Asgat) in toast, and whether it be Cheers, Santé, Salud, Probst, Skoal, Nasdarovia, Chin Chin, Namaste, In Lak'Ech, L'Chaim or Bilhana Woshefer, it is to our health, the collective health of the Sesh, all people, all from the same Mother Land and all with an inherent destiny to know the 360 Neters by name, and all with the innate ability to be as we were all intended to be—all Gods and Goddesses.

The light surrounds me,
The light comes through me,
I am the light.[2]

POSTSCRIPT

....

Even as I was working on preparing a final draft of this book, information shedding more light on these new paradigms kept pouring in at an unprecedented rate. In August of 1999, Dr. Zahi Hawass and the Egyptian Supreme Council of Antiquities announced the news of a spectacular archaeological find, a cache of mummies located at the Bahariya Oasis in the Western Desert.

The site was first discovered three years earlier, but excavations were not begun until March of 1999. Hawass made the announcement to the world in August and stated that 105 mummies had been uncovered, many still in their gold gilded anthropomorphic cartonnages (coffins painted with a likeness of the deceased). This was a common practice in the Greco-Roman era of Khemitian history, and most of these mummies will probably date from 200 BC to AD 200, the so called Late Period, the end of dynastic Khemit. Hawass also announced there may be up to 10,000 people buried at this site, which indicates an extensive necropolis. More important as pertaining to the new paradigms presented in this book, Hawass also stated that the ancient site at Bahariya was much greater than ever before believed. Once again, I believe this indicates that the Greeks and Romans chose to bury their dead, like the dynastic Khemitians, at the ancient sites of the previous predynastic Khemitian civilization. I propose that further excavations at all the Oases will reveal remnants of the ancient Khemitian Per-Bas, proving that the Ptolemaic Greeks and later Romans settled near and created their burial sites at sacred ancient Khemitian areas, once again to identify with the earlier civilization and its greatness.

The Bahariya find was further presented to the world in the second Fox TV broadcast in Egypt and aired live on May 23, 2000. On this second show, Dr. Zahi Hawass brought viewers into the tombs at the Bahariya oasis. This find is the greatest in Hawass's career, and he was overjoyed at what was presented live to the whole world. What was important for us, in light of our new paradigms, was the crude condition of the stone sarcophagi uncovered. Using the standard chronology of Egyptology that only 2000 years or so had passed from the supposed stone technology of the "Pyramid Age" of the 4th Dynasty of the Old Kingdom Period (ca. 2500 BC), the Ptolemaic Khemitians (330-30 BC) had lost all knowledge of fine drilling, cutting and precise shaping of hard stone. Of course, I contend that the Old Kingdom Khemitians could not cut at the precision and tolerances exhibited at Giza and the other Bu Wizzer sites either and inherited those stone structures from the ancient Khemitians.

In mid 1999 the orthodox Egyptology community decided to respond to the increased acceptance and positive popular as well as professional reaction to Christopher Dunn's work. As Dunn has reported, not only the general public but many professionals, including engineers of all specializations, NASA scientists, stone masons, architects, and even theoretical physicists, have voiced great positive reactions to his theories. Academic Egyptology, in the person of Mark Lehner, has decided they can no longer ignore Dunn's work, and they must launch a "counter offensive" to defend their dying paradigms. Lehner returned to Egypt in 1999 to film another documentary for NOVA and PBS. Lehner has once more employed stone mason Roger Hopkins to attempt to demonstrate that indeed the dynastic Khemitians could cut granite with copper chisels and drills.

Christopher Dunn and I have had many discussions about the Egyptologists' efforts to show that the ancient Khemitians did not need to employ advanced machining techniques to build the Per-Neters and Per-Bas, that the use of copper chisels and drills with a sand grit could indeed effectively cut into granite and basalt. Dunn remains adamant in defending his thesis, and we both propose a challenge for Egyptologists and the public alike: it is one thing to demonstrate that granite can be cut with copper tools utilizing a diamond or quartz sand grit. It is quite another thing to demonstrate the exact level of precision and tolerances exhibited in the Per-Neters and Per-Bas of the ancient Khemitians. When and if Lehner and Hopkins can demonstrate multiple contoured angles and tolerances of 2/10,000 of an inch in granite, basalt, schist and alabaster with copper chisels and drills, then we will really stand up and take notice!

Amazingly, information keeps arising that adds credence to our new paradigms.

While in the process of compiling this book, I was finishing the reading of another excellent book, *The Mystery of the Crystal Skulls*, written by Chris Morton and Ceri Thomas in 1997. Since I have also been involved in researching crystal skulls since 1979, this book was a must for me to read. In their book, Morton and Thomas relate the findings of scientists Lars Stixrude of the University of Gottingen and Ronald Cohen of the Carnegie Institution that the center of the Earth is a solid crystal 744 miles across.[1] Certainly, this adds more credence to Christopher Dunn's view that the Great Pyramid acted as a coupled oscillator and that the Earth is crystalline in its nature. Here is another fact discovered as "new" that probably was known to the ancient Khemitians.

The most exciting current news for me, as pertaining to the major theme of this work, that of the ancient Khemitian's knowledge and utilization of water, is the recent work done by other researchers in this area. In April of 1999, I was a presenter at Dr. Chet Snow's Crystal Skull Conference in Sedona, Arizona. The keynote speaker was Dr. G. Pat Flanagan, author of the book *Pyramid Power*, who spoke about his recent discoveries of and work with what has become known as "Hunza Water." The Hunza people are well known for their outstanding good health and longevity, most individuals living well over 100 years. Flanagan found that the water the Hunza drink is full of colloidal minerals and dissolved carbons, and he believed that it was this water that has been the secret to their good health and longevity, true to the teachings of Viktor Schauberger and Johann Grander. I discussed with Dr. Flanagan my new paradigms as well as the use of water for energy by the ancient Khemitians, and he was quite interested in my work.

In May of 1999, Drunvalo Melchizedek was the keynote speaker at the Wesak Festival in Mt. Shasta, California. Among other things, Drunvalo spoke of some "miracle" water discovered in Turkey, known to a group of Sufis in the region. Besides maintaining good health and longevity, this water has demonstrated the ability to "cure" polluted water and return it to its pristine state. Drunvalo announced that the Sufis have decided to release this water to the general public to help alleviate and reverse the global environmental crisis of polluted water supplies. I cannot help but think that these Turkish Sufis may be part of the indigenous tradition, the keepers of the written Khemitian Suf language and the wisdom of the ancient Khemitian knowledge of water. On his website Drunvalo has stated he will continue his research into this miracle water and will provide future updates for all interested. Many other researchers and scientists are currently very active in water research, and this work will continue to increase our collective understanding of the fluid of life we call water.

Finally (at least for now), at the annual conference of the Geological Society of America held in Reno, Nevada in November 2000, Dr. Robert Schoch and John Anthony West presented a paper entitled "Further Evidence Supporting a Pre-2500 BC Date for the Great Sphinx of Giza, Egypt." Among other things, Schoch and West presented evidence of a water-eroded lower chamber in the Red Pyramid at Dahshur (*see* Figure 89). West and Schoch maintain this chamber was constructed in predynastic times and the upper chambers built on top of it.[2] I, of course, would maintain the whole Per-Neter was constructed in predynastic times and the water erosion in the lower chamber is evidence of the water used for harmonic acoustic resonance. But this presentation did much to add more evidence for the existence of the ancient Khemitian culture and their uses of water.

More evidence will continue to come in as 2001 is a year predicted by many to be a "Year of Unveiling." As the new Kheper, the dawn of consciousness approaches, more of the ancient wisdom and knowledge will become known consciously to us all.

Figure 89.
Dahshur. Red Pyramid. Lower chamber shows evidence of water erosion, also mentioned by John Anthony West and Dr. Robert Schoch. 1997. Photo by author.

APPENDIX A

....

MAYAN INICIATIC TOURS
S.A. DE C.V.

PASEO DE MONTEJO 481 DEPTO. 208 ● MERIDA, C.P. 97000 YUC. MEXICO
TEL. (99) 20-23-28 FAX (99) 20-19-12 E-MAIL mayan@mer1.uninet.net.mx

November 21, 1997

Mr. Stephen S. Mehler, M.A.
THE KINNAMAN FOUNDATION
3305 Austin Bluffs Parkway #13
Colorado Springs, CO 80918

Dear Mr. Mehler:

May the Great Father Sun be with you as you receive this letter.

Thank you for the interesting photographs which you were kind enough to send me. I regret that I was not able to participate in the Prophets Conference that took place in Phoenix, Arizona.

For most researchers it is difficult to accept that at some time in the past the Maya and the Egyptians had any communication, and some place these ancient cultures in different dates.

Let us see what the Maya language yields. To the best of my knowledge, the architect who designed and built the Pyramid of Zakkara was Inhotep. In the Maya Itza language, INHOTEP means: IN - Indicative of first person, I. HO - Emerge and TEP is the root of TEPEU, one of the creators mentioned in the Popol Vuh, the sacred book of the Maya.

Furthermore, it turns out to be that K'UFU is the real name of the pyramid of KEOPS. K'U means GOD in Maya Itza or sacred area. As you can see, there are many indications to the effect that at some time the Maya were in Egypt and that in another time the Egyptians were in the land of the Maya.

MAYA MYSTERIES SCHOOL • MAYAN INITIATION CENTERS • CENTER FOR MAYAN STUDIES

MAYAN INICIATIC TOURS
S.A. DE C.V.

PASEO DE MONTEJO 481 DEPTO. 208 ● MERIDA, C.P. 97000 YUC. MEXICO
TEL. (99) 20-23-28 FAX (99) 20-19-12 E-MAIL mayan@mer1.uninet.net.mx

Mr. Stephen S. Mehler - Page 2

The glyphs on the ceiling shown in the photograph which you sent me definitely look Maya in their colors, graphic structure and sequence, Even as it was hard to read them, I could identify two of them.

Thank you for conveying Barbara Hand Clow's regards to me. Most probably she will be visiting the land of the Maya next year.

Attached is information on the the events that will take place in the spring of 1998 in this sacred land of the Maya.

May the Great Spirit be with you always.

Hunbatz Men
Maya Tradition

MAYA MYSTERIES SCHOOL • MAYAN INITIATION CENTERS • CENTER FOR MAYAN STUDIES

APPENDIX B

....

By Christopher Dunn

The ancient Egyptians were great manufacturers. Take this as a fact. From a distant epoch in prehistory to today, manufacturing has always been in a constant state of revolution, with old ideas being tossed aside in an attempt to beat competition and remain viable. The relationship between academia and manufacturing is a symbiotic one. While high level research and development feeds many elements found in manufacturing, businesses advise schools on what skills need to be taught to students who will be entering the job market. When schools cannot produce the textbooks from which workers learn, companies look elsewhere for help.

The world of manufacturing has brought tremendous progress to our civilization. In terms of generating wealth, no other human endeavor has the same impact as manufacturing. Having spent over 40 years working with machine-tools at various levels in industry, I recognize that one who is not familiar with the life of an engineer or technologist may view practitioners within the machine trades as somewhat mechanistic and devoid of spirit. Such, however, is not the case. You will find within manufacturing companies people with spirit and passion—people who are great philosophers and who can hold their own in any political or religious debate.

After reading my final manuscript for *The Giza Power Plant*, Stephen Mehler expressed a concern that I did not bring more personal experiences and philosophy to its pages. In retrospect, I wish I had, but my decision not to was so that hard facts and details I brought forward in that book could not be dismissed because of subjective and unverifiable data. One remarkable fateful conclusion that I had reached in writing *The Giza*

Power Plant was that I was not equipped to explain when and by whom the pyramids were built. My inclinations were that the pyramids were older than conventional teachings tell us, but in the face of contradiction, I didn't believe I could adequately defend such a position. I am particularly pleased that *The Land Of Osiris* is now published, because it adds a vital link to the puzzle that is ancient Egypt—or Khemit. Before my own book *The Giza Power Plant* was published, I had no idea if, when, or where support for what is proposed within its pages would come from. I was delighted, therefore, to learn from Stephen Mehler that the indigenous teachings of ancient Khemit substantially supported what I have proposed.

Nevertheless, even with the support of the indigenous teachers of Egypt there are many aspects of my work that need attention in order for these ideas to filter into the Western mind. Continued research in the machining methods used by the Egyptians is one. It seems that as long as armchair theorists can imagine the creation of an object using sand and copper, any objection to such technically vacuous notions is met with the standard explanation that time is all that is needed. Oh, you wouldn't be able to create these objects in a 20 year period. Fine, throw another 20 years onto it. Or 1,000 years if necessary. As long as I don't have to question what I have been taught in school.

If I sound somewhat cynical, it is because I have been faced with clever sophists who have never been to Egypt, do not have an understanding of what I have learned during my 40 year career, but can cite historic source material like scriptures on a Sunday.

More work needs to be done. When Stephen Mehler and I were wandering the Giza Plateau in May 1999, it became clear to us that our own particular backgrounds combined present a forceful argument that in isolation would not hold the same weight. Stephen's dedication to learning the oral tradition that has been passed down from generation to generation is vital to our understanding of the ancient pyramid builders. In his previous visit, Stephen had gone looking for the contoured block of granite that I describe in *The Giza Power Plant*. As we headed south past the Great Pyramid, he started to veer toward the East.

"Where are you going?" I asked.

"To the contoured block of granite!" he replied.

"Are you sure?" I asked, somewhat confused as to why he was heading in the wrong direction.

"Of course!" he said striding along.

Stephen's block of granite was not the same one that I describe in my book. It is MUCH more impressive and I can't wait to get back there with the proper instruments to check it out (*see* Figure 8, page 36). I later showed him the block that I had described in my book.

There is more work to be done in the Serapeum, if I can gain permission to go back in there, and the boxes in the pyramid need another range of tests that will further confirm what I had measured using rudimentary instruments in prior visits. Though unable to access the Serapeum, I was able to verify additional feats of amazing precision in the box in Khafre's Pyramid. On this trip to Egypt, I took along a toolmaker's precision square. I was stricken with disbelief when I placed the square against the inside corner of the box. I was expecting it to be fairly close, but I did not expect it to be perfectly square. On three corners there was no deviation from squareness. On one corner there was a sliver of light showing where the square deviated slightly.

Of no less importance, on inspecting the corner radius on this box, I found it to be an amazing 1/8-inch radius!

These discoveries are significant for they emphasize the question why? Why was it necessary to create this box with perfectly square corners? Why was it important to have such a small radius on the inside corner? We have been treated to images of ancient Egyptians bashing granite using dolorite balls. This quality of work far surpasses the work a dolorite ball can accomplish—regardless of the skill of the worker.

Creating beautiful objects in reverence to a king is not unusual. However, creating starkly utilitarian objects with such a high order of precision speaks of technologies and purposes that are only attributed to the ancient Egyptians, or Khemitians, in their oral traditions.

As my parents would say to me: "Listen to your Elders, and respect what they have to say."

ENDNOTES

....

Introduction

[1] These three questions are posed as one in J.G. Bennett, *Gurdjieff: Making a New World*, 184.

Chapter One

[1] It is interesting to note that Abd'El means "servant" or "slave," and Hakim means "wisdom." He is indeed a servant to wisdom. Awyan is the formal name of the Awayani Tribe, called the "Eye" people.

[2] This theme will be explored in much greater detail in my second book, now in progress.

[3] John Anthony West, *Serpent in the Sky*, 198.

[4] Murry Hope, *Ancient Egypt: The Sirius Connection*, 58. I cannot overemphasize the importance of this book for my inspiration to find the indigenous teachings of Egypt.

Chapter Two

[1] In the University of California, Berkeley, Anthropology Library in 1993 we found a complete set of the original *American Antiquarian and Oriental Journal* and verified Kinnaman's connections to and editorship of the periodical.

[2] Willi Semple, "Dr. Kinnaman: Digger for Facts," 259.

[3] J.O. Kinnaman, *The Great Pyramid*, 23.

[4] Refer to Thomas Hale, *Griots and Griottes*, for a more extensive treatment of this subject.

Chapter Three

[1] Peter Tompkins, *Secrets of the Great Pyramid*, 2-3.

[2] Some of these excerpts can be found in G.R.S. Mead, *Thrice Greatest Hermes*.

[3] Many of the Arab chronicles and histories can be found in the works of Joseph Jochmans.

[4] Often ignored by many writers who credit Champollion with solely deciphering the hieroglyphs is the fact that British scholar Thomas Young also worked independently on translations for many years. Some British authors claim Champollion borrowed liberally from Young's work and did not give him proper credit.

Chapter Four

[1] Thomas S. Kuhn, *The Structure of Scientific Revolutions*, 84-85.

[2] Ibid, 175.

[3] In the preface to the second edition of his book, Professor Kuhn discussed the adverse reaction to his theory by social scientists and addresses his critics.

[4] Dennis Brian, *Einstein: A Life*, 60-62.

[5] Mark Lehner, *The Complete Pyramids*, 38-39.

[6] Ibid, 39.

[7] Ibid, 25.

[8] See the works of both Isha and R.A. Schwaller de Lubicz for a more detailed discussion of this point.

Chapter Five

[1] Margaret Murray, *The Splendor that was Egypt*, 100.

[2] This book is an excellent source to establish the ideas presented in this book. It was only many years after she was out of academia that Dr. Murray was able to freely discuss the sexism and rigidity in thinking that she had experienced in her academic career.

[3] R. A. Schwaller de Lubicz, *Sacred Science*, 3, 77, 162-166, 208.

[4] Lehner, *The Complete Pyramids*, 34.

[5] Christopher Dunn, *The Giza Power Plant*, 138-139.

[6] See article by V. Krasnoholovets on the website www.gizapyramid.com, research articles.

[7] A research colleague, Chuck Putnam, has provided a corroborative link to Hakim's date of over 65,000 years ago as the beginning of the current Khemitian cycle. In Maurice Chatelain's, *Our Cosmic Ancestors*, in the chapter entitled "The Constant of Ninevah," the author discusses the find in the ruins of an Assyrian library at Ninevah, a number that is given special significance. This number is referred to as a special beginning date which Chatelain calculates as being 64,800 years ago, 27-45.

[8] *Oxford English Dictionary*, Vol. II, 113.

[9] Ibid, Vol. I, 183.

Chapter Six

[1] Recorded statements by Mark Lehner in the video, Mysteries of the Sphinx, BC Productions, 1993.

[2] The term *Ur Nil* was first coined by German scientist M.L.P. Blanckenhorn. Michael Hoffman, *Egypt Before The Pharaohs*, 28.

Chapter Seven

[1] Peter Clayton, *Chronicle of the Pharaohs*, 42-45.

[2] Lehner, *The Complete Pyramids*, 101-105.

Chapter Eight
[1] Lehner, *The Complete Pyramids*, 82-93.
[2] Ibid, 88.
[3] John Anthony West, *The Travelers Key To Ancient Egypt*, 190-191.
[4] Dunn, *The Giza Power Plant*, 96-97.

Chapter Nine
[1] Clayton, *Chronicle of the Pharaohs*, 60-62.
[2] Lehner, *The Complete Pyramids*, 142.
[3] *Oxford English Dictionary*, Vol. I, 1962.
[4] Clayton, *Chronicle of the Pharaohs*, 61.
[5] Kinnaman, *The Great Pyramid*, 33.
[6] Lehner, *The Complete Pyramids*, 152.

Chapter Ten
[1] Lehner, *The Complete Pyramids*, 95.
[2] Drunvalo Melchizedek, *The Ancient Secret of The Flower of Life*, Vol. I, 125.

Chapter Eleven
[1] Lehner, *The Complete Pyramids*, 106-119.
[2] See video Mysteries of the Sphinx.
[3] See Appendix A for complete letter.
[4] Dr Zahi Hawass's website, http://guardians.net/hawass/osiris/.htm
[5] See website for The Great Pyramid of Giza Research Association, www.giza-pyramid.com, for alternative theories of the functions of the Great Pyramid, including an article by Dr. V. Krasnoholovets.
[6] See Dr. Schoch's website, http://robertschoch.homestead.com/main.html
[7] Lehner, *The Complete Pyramids*, 127-132.
[8] John Baines and Jaromir Malek, *Atlas of Ancient Egypt*, 1980, New York: Facts on File, 140.
[9] Dunn, *The Giza Power Plant*, 138, 219.
[10] Ibid, 204, 208, 238-239.
[11] Again, see Hawass's website.

Chapter Twelve
[1] Lehner, *The Complete Pyramids*, 120-121.

Chapter Thirteen
[1] Hoffman, *Egypt Before The Pharaohs*, 28.
[2] Ibid, 20, 28-29, 48, 58, 218.

³ Rushdie Said, *The Geological Evolution of The River Nile*, 7-9.
⁴ Coy H. Squyres et al., *Guidebook to the Geology and Archaeology of Egypt*, 100.

Chapter Fourteen
¹ Callum Coats, *Living Energies*, 46, 48-49.
² Ibid, 10-11. 276-278.
³ Hans Kronberger and Siegbert Lattacher, *On The Track of Water's Secret*, 30-31.
⁴ Coats, *Living Energies*, 10-11. 278.
⁵ Kronberger, *On The Track of Water's Secret*, 49-61.
⁶ Ibid, 62-64.
⁷ Ibid, 51.
⁸ Coats, *Living Energies*, 111.

Chapter Fifteen
¹ Mark Lehner, *The Egyptian Heritage*.
² David Hatcher Childress, *Lost Cities of North And Central America*, 316-325, 336-337.
³ Kinnaman, *The Great Pyramid*, 10-11.
⁴ G.I. Gurdjieff, *Meetings With Remarkable Men*, 97-100.
⁵ William Patrick Patterson, "Gurdjieff in Egypt", *Telos* Magazine, Vol. 2, No. 1-3.

Chapter Sixteen
¹ In some articles in journals, such as *KMT* Magazine, Egyptologists have referred to the blue pigments as oxides of copper but I have not seen any detailed spectrographic analysis presented to support this contention.
² Robert Bauval and Graham Hancock, *The Message of The Sphinx*, 249.
³ Jane B. Sellers, *The Death of Gods in Ancient Egypt*, 13.
⁴ Ibid, 39-40.
⁵ The term Wizzer is the origin of the Turkish word "Vizier" or "Wazzir", a term used by Egyptologists to refer to the person who was second in importance only to the king, and who handled all administrative functions in dynastic Khemit. The word "wisdom" may be directly derived from Wizzer also.
⁶ E. A. Reymond, *The Origins of the Egyptian Temple*, 12-13, 55, 118.
⁷ Ibid, 118-119.
⁸ Melchizedek, *The Ancient Secret of the Flower of Life*, Vol. I, 207-209.

Chapter Seventeen
¹ Malidoma Patrice Somé, *The Healing Wisdom of Africa*, 218-219.
² Ancient Khemitian prayer as translated into English by Abd'El Hakim Awyan.

Postscript
1 Chris Morton and Ceri Thomas, *The Mystery of the Crystal Skulls*, 274.
2 *Atlantis Rising* Magazine, No. 26, 10.

SELECTED REFERENCES

....

Adams, W. Marsham. *The Book Of The Master of The Hidden Places.* Surrey: The Aquarian Press, Ltd, 1980 (1933).

Allan, D. S. and J. B Delair. *Cataclysm!* Santa Fe: Bear & Co, 1987.

Amen, Nur Ankh. *The Ankh.* New York: Lushena Books, 1993.

Asante, Molefi Kete. *The Egyptian Philosophers.* Chicago: African American Images, 2000.

Aziz, Phillipe. *The Mysteries of The Great Pyramid.* Geneva: Editions Ferni, 1977.

Bauval, Robert and Adrian Gilbert. *The Orion Mystery.* New York: Crown Publishers, 1994.

_____ and Graham Hancock. *The Message Of The Sphinx.* New York: Crown Publishers, 1996.

ben-Jochannan, Yosef. *African Origin Of The Major "Western Religions."* Baltimore: Black Classic Press, 1991 (1970).

Bennett, J. G. *Gurdjieff: Making A New World.* New York: Harper & Row, 1973.

Bernal, Martin. *Black Athena.* New Brunswick: Rutgers University Press, 1987.

Billard, Jules, ed. *Ancient Egypt: Discovering Its Splendors.* Washington, D.C.: National Geographic Society, 1978.

Blavatsky, H. P. *The Secret Doctrine* Vol. II. Pasadena: Theosophical University Press, 1970 (1888).

Bowen, Sandra, F. R. Nocerino, and Joshua Shapiro. *Mysteries Of The Crystal Skulls Revealed.* Pacifican: J&S Aquarian Networking, 1988.

Bramley, William. *The Gods Of Eden.* San Jose: Dahlin Family Press, 1989.

Breasted, J. H. *A History Of Egypt.* New York: Scribners & Sons, 1909.

_____. *Ancient Records of Egypt* Vol. I. New York: Russell & Russell. 1962 (1906).

Brian, Dennis. *Einstein: A Life.* New York: John Wiley & Sons, 1996.

Bridges, Marilyn. *Egypt: Antiquities From Above.* Boston: Little, Brown and Company, 1996.

Brier, Bob. *Ancient Egyptian Magic.* New York: William Morrow & Co, 1980.

Bromage, Bernard. *The Occult Arts of Ancient Egypt.* New York: The Aquarian Press, 1960 (1953).

Brunton, Paul. *A Search in Secret Egypt*. New York: Samuel Wiser, Inc, 1977 (1935).

Budge, E. A. Wallis. *The Egyptian Book of The Dead*. New York: Dover Publications, 1967 (1895).

_____. *Osiris* Vol. I & II. New York: Dover Publications, 1973. (1911).

Burgoyne, Thomas H. *The Light of Egypt* Vol. I & II. Denver: H. O.Wagner, 1965 (1889).

Cayce, Edgar E. *Edgar Cayce on Atlantis*. New York: Warner Books, Inc, 1968.

Chatelain, Maurice. *Our Cosmic Ancestors*. Sedona: Temple Golden Publications, 1988n (1975).

Childress, David Hatcher. *Lost Cities of Arabia & Africa*. Kempton: Adventures Unlimited Press, 1989.

_____. *Lost Cities of North & Central America*. Kempton: Adventures Unlimited Press, 1992.

Clayton, Peter A. *A Chronicle Of The Pharaohs*. London: Thames and Hudson, Ltd, 1994.

Clow, Barbara Hand. *The Pleiadian Agenda*. Santa Fe: Bear & Co, 1995.

Coats, Callum. *Living Energies*. Bath: Gateway Books, 1996.

Cottrell, Leonard. *Life Under The Pharaohs*. New York: Holt, Rinehart and Winston, 1960.

Cremo, Michael and Richard Thompson. *The Hidden History Of The Human Race*. Badger: Govardhan Hill Publishing, 1994.

Davidovits, Joseph and Margie Morris. *The Pyramids: An Enigma Solved*. New York: Dorset Press, 1988.

Desroches-Noblecourt, Christiane. *Tutankhamen*. Boston: New York Graphic Society, 1963.

Diop, Cheikh Anta. *The African Origin of Civilization*. New York: Lawrence Hill, 1974.

D'Olivet, Fabre. *The Hebraic Tongue Restored*. York Beach: Samuel Weiser, Inc, 1981 (1921, 1815).

Drower, Margaret S. *Flinders Petrie: A Life in Archaeology*. London: Victor Gollancz, Ltd., 1985.

Dunn, Christopher. *The Giza Power Plant*. Santa Fe: Bear & Co, 1998.

Edwards, I. E. S. *The Pyramids of Egypt*. London: Penguin Books, 1993 (1969).

Ellis, Normandie. *Awakening Osiris*. Ann Arbor: Phanes Press, 1988.

El Mahdy, Christine. *Mummies, Myth and Magic*. London: Thames and Hudson, Inc, 1989.

Selected References

Emory, Walter B. *Archaic Egypt*. New York: Penguin Books, 1962.

Fakhry, Ahmed. *The Pyramids*. Chicago: U. of Chicago Press, 1961.

Flindt, Max and Otto Binder. *Mankind-Child of The Stars*. Greenwich: Fawcett Publications, 1974.

Freer, Neil. *Breaking The Godspell*. Phoenix: New Falcon Publications, 1987.

Freud, Sigmund. *Moses and Monotheism*. New York: Vintage Books, 1939.

Guilmot, Max. *The Initiatory Process In Ancient Egypt*. San Jose: AMORC, 1978.

Gurdjieff, G.I. *Meetings With Remarkable Men*. New York: Penguin Books, 1985 (1960).

Hale, Thomas A. *Griots And Griottes*. Indianapolis: Indiana University Press, 1998.

Hancock, Graham. *Fingerprints Of The Gods*. New York: Crown Publishers, 1995.

_____. *Heavens Mirror*. New York: Three Rivers Press, 1998.

Hapgood, Charles H. *Maps of The Ancient Sea Kings*. Kempton: Adventures Unlimited Press, 1996 (1966).

Hoffman, Michael A. *Egypt Before The Pharaohs*. London: Michael O'Mara Books Limited, 1991 (1979).

Holt, Erika. *The Sphinx and The Great Pyramid*. Los Angeles: Summit University Press, 1968.

Hope, Murry. *The Lion People*. Devon: Thoth Publications, 1988.

_____. *Ancient Egypt: The Sirius Connection*. Dorset: Element Books Limited, 1990.

_____. *The Paschats and the Crystal People*. Leicestershire: Thoth Publications, 1992.

_____. *The Ancient Wisdom of Egypt*. London: Thorsons, 1998 (1984).

Horn, Arthur David. *Humanity's Extraterrestrial Origins*. Mount Shasta: A&L Horn, 1994.

Hurry, Jamieson B. *Imhotep*. Chicago: Ares Publishers, 1926.

Jairazbhoy, R. A. *Ancient Egyptian Survival In The Pacific*. London: Karnak House, 1990.

Jochmans, Joseph R. *Time-Capsule* Vol 1-4. Rock Hill: Alma Tara Publishing, 1993-1994.

Kinnaman, J. O. *The Great Pyramid*. Cambridge: Persuasive Press, 1999 (1940).

Knight, Christopher and Robert Lomas. *The Hiram Key*. New York: Barnes & Noble, 1996.

Kronberger, Hans and Siegbert Lattacher. *On The Track of Water's Secret*. Scottsdale: Wishland Publishing, Inc, 1995.

Kuhn, Thomas S. *The Structure Of Scientific Revolutions*. Chicago: The University of Chicago Press, 1970 (1962).

Lamy, Lucie. *Egyptian Mysteries*. New York: Crossroad Publishing Co, 1981.

LaViolette, Paul. *Earth Under Fire*. New York: Starlane Publishing, 1997.

Lehner, Mark. *The Egyptian Heritage*. Virginia Beach: ARE Press, 1974.

_____. *The Complete Pyramids*. London: Thames and Hudson, 1997.

Lesko, Barbara S. *The Remarkable Women of Ancient Egypt*. Berkeley: B.C. Scribe Publications, 1978.

_____. *The Great Goddesses Of Egypt*. Norman: U. of Oklahoma Press, 1999.

Lewis, H. Spencer. *The Symbolic Prophecy of The Great Pyramid*. San Jose: AMORC, 1957 (1936).

Mead, G. R. S. *Thrice Greatest Hermes*. York Beach: Samuel Weiser, Inc, 1992 (1906).

Mehler, Stephen S. "New View of Sphinx & Pyramids Age". *Rosicrucian Digest*. Vol. 71, No. 4 (p.16-20), Winter 1993.

_____. "Lifting The Veil: Speculation On The Face Of The Great Sphinx of Giza". *World Explorer Magazine*. Vol 1. No. 6, (p.38-41), 1995.

_____. "J. O. Kinnaman: Digger of Facts". *World Explorer Magazine*. Vol. 1, No. 7 (p.50-54), 1995.

_____."The Search For Kinnaman's Entrance". *Atlantis Rising Magazine*. Vol. 1, No.10 (p.35, 66-69), 1997.

_____. "The Search For Kinnaman's Entrance Continues...". *Atlantis Rising Magazine*. Vol. 1, No. 14 (p.20, 22, 57), 1998.

Melchizedek, Drunvalo. *The Ancient Secret Of The Flower Of Life*. Vol. I & II. Sedona: Light Technology Publishing, 1998, 2000.

Men, Hunbatz. *Secrets of Mayan Science/Religion*. Santa Fe: Bear & Co., 1990.

Mendelssohn, Kurt. *The Pyramids of Egypt*. New York: Praeger, 1974.

Michalowski, Kazimierz. *Art of Ancient Egypt*. New York: Harry N. Abrams, Inc., 1980.

Morton, Chris and Ceri L. Thomas. *The Mystery of The Crystal Skulls*. Santa Fe: Bear & Co., 1998.

Murray, Margaret. *The Splendor That Was Egypt*. New York: Philosophical Library, 1961 (1949).

_____. *My First Hundred Years*. London: William Kimber, 1963.

Noone, Richard. *5/5/2000 Ice: The Ultimate Disaster*. New York: Harmony Books, 1986.

Osman, Ahmed. *Stranger in the Valley of the Kings*. San Francisco: Harper & Row, 1987.

Palmer, M. Dale. *True Esoteric Traditions*. Plainfield: Noetics Institute, Inc., 1994.

Petrie, W. M. Flinders. *A History of Egypt* Vol. I. London: Metheun & Co., 1903.

_____. *Seventy Years in Archaeology*. New York: Greenwood Press, 1969 (1932).

Pochan, Andre. *The Mysteries of The Great Pyramids*. New York: Avon Books, 1978 (1971).

Pye, Lloyd. *Everything You Know Is Wrong*. Madeira Beach: Adamu Press, 1997.

Reed, Bika. *Rebel In The Soul*. New York: Inner Traditions International, Ltd., 1978.

_____. *The Field of Transformations*. Rochester: Inner Traditions International, Ltd., 1987.

Reymond, E. A. E. *The Mythological Origin of The Egyptian Temple*. New York: Barnes & Noble, 1969.

Rolfe, Mona. *Initiation By The Nile*. London: Neville Spearman Limited, 1976.

Rux, Bruce. *Architects of The Underworld*. Berkeley: Frog, Ltd., 1996.

Said, Rushdie. *The Geological Evolution of the River Nile*. New York: Springer-Verlag, 1981.

Schoch, Robert M. "Redating The Great Sphinx". *KMT* Magazine. Vol. 3, No. 2 (p. 52-59, 66-70), Summer 1992.

Schwaller de Lubicz, Isha. *Her-Bak* Vol. I & II. New York: Inner Traditions International, Ltd., 1978 (1955).

Schwaller de Lubicz, R. A. *The Temple In Man*. Brookline: Autumn Press, 1977 (1949).

_____. *Sacred Science*. New York: Inner Traditions International, Ltd., 1982 (1961).

_____. *The Egyptian Miracle*. New York: Inner Traditions International, Ltd., 1985 (1963).

_____. *Esoterism and Symbol*. New York: Inner Traditions International, Ltd., 1985 (1960).

Sellers, Jane B. *The Death of Gods in Ancient Egypt*. New York: Penguin Books, 1992.

Semple, Willi W. "Dr. Kinnaman: Digger For Facts". *Rosicrucian Digest* Vol. 40, No.7. (p. 258-260). July 1962.

Sitchin, Zecharia. *The Stairway To Heaven*. New York: Avon Books, 1980.

_____. *The Wars of Gods and Men*. New York: Avon Books, 1985.

Smyth, Piazzi Charles. *The Great Pyramid*. New York: Bell Publishing Company, 1978 (1880).

Somé, Malidoma Patrice. *The Healing Wisdom of Africa*. New York: Putnam/Tarcher, 1999.

Squyres, Coy H. and Frank A. Reilly. *Guideline to the Geology and Archaeology of Egypt*. Petroleum Exploration Society of Libya: Sixth Annual Field Conference, 1964.

Steiner, Rudolf. *Egyptian Myths and Mysteries*. New York: Anthroposophic Press, Inc., 1971.

Stone, Merlin. *When God Was A Woman*. New York: Harcourt Brace Jovanovich, 1978.

Temple, Robert G. *The Sirius Mystery*. New York: Destiny Books, 1998.

Thompson, Gunnar. *American Discovery*. Seattle: Misty Isles Press, 1984.

Tompkins, Peter. *Secrets of The Great Pyramid*. New York: Harper Colophon Books, 1978 (1971).

_____. *The Magic of Obelisks*. New York: Harper & Row, 1981.

Vandenbroeck, Andre. *Al-Kemi*. Rochester: Inner Traditions International, Ltd., 1987.

Waddell, L. A. *Egyptian Civilization, Its Sumerian Origin and Real Chronology*. London: Luzac & Co., 1930.

Wenig, Steffen. *The Woman In Egyptian Art*. New York: McGraw-Hill Book Co., 1968.

West, John Anthony. *Serpent In The Sky*. New York: Harper & Row, 1979.

_____. *The Traveler's Key To Ancient Egypt*. Wheaton: Theosophical Publishing House, 1995 (1985).

Williamson, George H. *Secret Places of The Lion*. New York: Destiny Books, 1983 (1958).

Wolf, Fred Alan. *The Spiritual Universe*. Portsmouth: Moment Point Press, Inc., 1999.

Zink, David. *The Ancient Stones Speak*. New York: E.P. Dutton, 1979.

INDEX

....

metaphysics, 51, 160
mica, 151, 153, 200
Mit Rahaina, 40
Morton, Chris, 207, 220, 224
Moses and Monotheism, 223
Mousterian Subpluvial, 201
Murray, Margaret, 28, 42, 45, 217, 224
Mut, 116, 180
mysticism, 2, 4, 5, 147
myth, 24, 51, 159-160, 163-164, 171-174,
    188-189, 222
mythologue, 164
Naga Maya, 87, 194
Napoleon, 26, 55
National Geographic Magazine, xvi
Nazlet el Samman, iv, 20, 107, 196
Nefer, 120, 142, 146, 171, 203
Neith-Hotep, 117
Neter, 40, 48, 62, 88, 98, 110, 116, 137,
    165, 173, 180, 182, 186
Newton, Sir Isaac, 26
Nibiru, 176-178, 191
Nile Valley School, 54
Niuserre, 96
Nomes, 55
Noone, Richard, 155-158, 225
Nut, 52-53, 116, 182, 200
obelisk, *see also Ib Ra*, vii, xi, 95-98, 198-
    199
Offord, Henry, 19
Oon, 53
Orion, 88, 105, 183-184, 186, 188-189,
    190-192, 221
Osireion, x, 186-188
Osiris, *see also* Wizzer, v, x, xviii, 43-45,
    60, 62, 89, 106, 123-124, 173, 178,
    181, 184-186, 189, 213, 222
Osman, Ahmed, 57
paradigm shift, xviii, 31-32, 51, 195
Paschats, x, 181-182, 223
Patterson, William Patrick, 172-173, 188,
    219
Per-Aa, v, 42-43, 45, 123, 191
Per-Ba, v, 45-49, 88, 104, 120, 137, 169,
    185-186, 188, 203
Per-Ka, 45

Per-Neter, v, ix, 45, 47-50, 70, 72, 77, 91-
    92, 94, 98, 109, 113, 118, 120, 123-
    124, 128, 151-152, 155-157, 163,
    169, 191-192, 208
Petrie Museum, 17
Petrie, Sir Matthew Flinders, 14, 17-19,
    28, 35, 114, 156, 161, 169, 225
Pharaoh, v, 35, 42-43, 45, 144
Plato, 25, 159-160, 163-164, 188
Power Places Tours, iv, 10
Proctor, Joseph, 19
Ptah, x, 40, 178-179, 180, 184, 186, 190,
    200
Ptolemy, 25
Pye, Lloyd, 52, 176-177, 225
Pyramid Texts, 35, 87, 183-184, 186, 190
Pyramidos, 47-48
Pythagoras, 23, 186, 188
Qattara Depression, 138
Queen's Chamber, x, 152, 165, 167, 169
Ra, vii, 52-53, 97-98, 116
Red Pyramid, v, xi, 70-73, 208-209
Reed, Bika, 37
Reisner, George, 28, 114
Reymond, E. A., 173, 188-189, 219, 225
Roerich, Nicholas, 150
Rosetta Stone, 26, 37
Rosicrucian Order, AMORC, 181
Sa, 136
Sahu, 184
Sahura, vii, 92-94
Sakkara, vi, vii, ix, xviii, 35, 46, 60, 62, 75-
    78, 82-84, 87-88, 90, 96, 105, 109,
    128, 143, 157, 177, 186, 203
Sa-Ptah, 179, 184, 190
Saqqara, *see* Sakkara
sarcophagus, 89, 123-124, 168
Schauberger, Viktor, xviii, 18, 142, 144-
    150, 152-153, 158, 169, 171, 200,
    203, 207
Schauberger, Walter, 149
schist plates, ix, 157-158
Schoch, Robert M., xi, 59-60, 115-116,
    132, 208-209, 218, 225
Schwaller de Lubicz, Isha, 37
Schwaller de Lubicz, R. A., 29, 37, 48, 52,

Index

ABOUT THE AUTHOR

....

Stephen S. Mehler's fascination with Egypt, which began at the age of eight, has guided his education and spiritual work all his life. Born in Brooklyn and raised in the Bronx, Mehler studied physiology and anatomy at Hunter College of the City University of New York. He holds two masters degrees from San Jose State University in the natural and social sciences. Pursuing metaphysical as well as scientific truth, Mehler served as a staff research scientist for the Rosicrucian Order, AMORC from 1978 to 1980, and was a professional astrologer and lecturer on Egypt and the ancient crystal skulls connected to the Maya of Mexico and Central America. Stephen has studied material about ancient Egypt for over 33 years.

In his research, Mehler discovered hints that an ancient, hidden tradition still survived in Egypt, one that predated even the dynastic civilization, a group that had kept alive the secrets of the ancients. Traveling to Egypt in search of this indigenous wisdom, at the foot of the Sphinx Mehler found this knowledge embodied in a living teacher, Abd'El Hakim Awyan. *The Land of Osiris: An Introduction to Khemitology* takes us with Mehler on his fascinating journey and reveals this knowledge that has been kept secret all these years, kept safe so that it can be revealed now, at the Dawn of the new age.

ANCIENT ALIENS ON THE MOON
By Mike Bara
What did NASA find in their explorations of the solar system that they may have kept from the general public? How ancient really are these ruins on the Moon? Using official NASA and Russian photos of the Moon, Bara looks at vast cityscapes and domes in the Sinus Medii region as well as glass domes in the Crisium region. Bara also takes a detailed look at the mission of Apollo 17 and the case that this was a salvage mission, primarily concerned with investigating an opening into a massive hexagonal ruin near the landing site. Chapters include: The History of Lunar Anomalies; The Early 20th Century; Sinus Medii; To the Moon Alice!; Mare Crisium; Yes, Virginia, We Really Went to the Moon; Apollo 17; more. Tons of photos of the Moon examined for possible structures and other anomalies.
248 Pages. 6x9 Paperback. Illustrated.. $19.95. Code: AAOM

ANCIENT ALIENS ON MARS
By Mike Bara
Bara brings us this lavishly illustrated volume on alien structures on Mars. Was there once a vast, technologically advanced civilization on Mars, and did it leave evidence of its existence behind for humans to find eons later? Did these advanced extraterrestrial visitors vanish in a solar system wide cataclysm of their own making, only to make their way to Earth and start anew? Was Mars once as lush and green as the Earth, and teeming with life? Chapters include: War of the Worlds; The Mars Tidal Model; The Death of Mars; Cydonia and the Face on Mars; The Monuments of Mars; The Search for Life on Mars; The True Colors of Mars and The Pathfinder Sphinx; more. Color section.
252 Pages. 6x9 Paperback. Illustrated. $19.95. Code: AMAR

ANCIENT TECHNOLOGY IN PERU & BOLIVIA
By David Hatcher Childress
Childress speculates on the existence of a sunken city in Lake Titicaca and reveals new evidence that the Sumerians may have arrived in South America 4,000 years ago. He demonstrates that the use of "keystone cuts" with metal clamps poured into them to secure megalithic construction was an advanced technology used all over the world, from the Andes to Egypt, Greece and Southeast Asia. He maintains that only power tools could have made the intricate articulation and drill holes found in extremely hard granite and basalt blocks in Bolivia and Peru, and that the megalith builders had to have had advanced methods for moving and stacking gigantic blocks of stone, some weighing over 100 tons.
340 Pages. 6x9 Paperback. Illustrated.. $19.95 Code: ATP

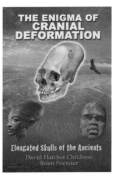

THE ENIGMA OF CRANIAL DEFORMATION
Elongated Skulls of the Ancients
By David Hatcher Childress and Brien Foerster
In a book filled with over a hundred astonishing photos and a color photo section, Childress and Foerster take us to Peru, Bolivia, Egypt, Malta, China, Mexico and other places in search of strange elongated skulls and other cranial deformation. The puzzle of why diverse ancient people—even on remote Pacific Islands—would use head-binding to create elongated heads is mystifying. Where did they even get this idea? Did some people naturally look this way—with long narrow heads? Were they some alien race? Were they an elite race that roamed the entire planet? Why do anthropologists rarely talk about cranial deformation and know so little about it?
250 Pages. 6x9 Paperback. Illustrated. $19.95. Code: ECD

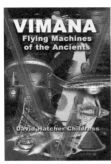

VIMANA:
Flying Machines of the Ancients
by David Hatcher Childress

According to early Sanskrit texts the ancients had several types of airships called vimanas. Like aircraft of today, vimanas were used to fly through the air from city to city; to conduct aerial surveys of uncharted lands; and as delivery vehicles for awesome weapons. David Hatcher Childress, popular *Lost Cities* author and star of the History Channel's long-running show Ancient Aliens, takes us on an astounding investigation into tales of ancient flying machines. In his new book, packed with photos and diagrams, he consults ancient texts and modern stories and presents astonishing evidence that aircraft, similar to the ones we use today, were used thousands of years ago in India, Sumeria, China and other countries. Includes a 24-page color section.

408 Pages. 6x9 Paperback. Illustrated. $22.95. Code: VMA

LOST CITIES OF ATLANTIS, ANCIENT EUROPE & THE MEDITERRANEAN
by David Hatcher Childress

Childress takes the reader in search of sunken cities in the Mediterranean; across the Atlas Mountains in search of Atlantean ruins; to remote islands in search of megalithic ruins; to meet living legends and secret societies. From Ireland to Turkey, Morocco to Eastern Europe, and around the remote islands of the Mediterranean and Atlantic, Childress takes the reader on an astonishing quest for mankind's past. Ancient technology, cataclysms, megalithic construction, lost civilizations and devastating wars of the past are all explored in this book.

524 PAGES. 6x9 PAPERBACK. ILLUSTRATED. $16.95. CODE: MED

LOST CITIES OF CHINA, CENTRAL ASIA & INDIA
by David Hatcher Childress

Like a real life "Indiana Jones," maverick archaeologist David Childress takes the reader on an incredible adventure across some of the world's oldest and most remote countries in search of lost cities and ancient mysteries. Discover ancient cities in the Gobi Desert; hear fantastic tales of lost continents, vanished civilizations and secret societies bent on ruling the world; visit forgotten monasteries in forbidding snow-capped mountains with strange tunnels to mysterious subterranean cities! A unique combination of far-out exploration and practical travel advice, it will astound and delight the experienced traveler or the armchair voyager.

429 PAGES. 6x9 PAPERBACK. ILLUSTRATED. FOOTNOTES & BIBLIOGRAPHY. $14.95. CODE: CHI

LOST CITIES OF ANCIENT LEMURIA & THE PACIFIC
by David Hatcher Childress

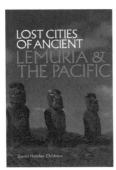

Was there once a continent in the Pacific? Called Lemuria or Pacifica by geologists, Mu or Pan by the mystics, there is now ample mythological, geological and archaeological evidence to "prove" that an advanced and ancient civilization once lived in the central Pacific. Maverick archaeologist and explorer David Hatcher Childress combs the Indian Ocean, Australia and the Pacific in search of the surprising truth about mankind's past. Contains photos of the underwater city on Pohnpei; explanations on how the statues were levitated around Easter Island in a clockwise vortex movement; tales of disappearing islands; Egyptians in Australia; and more.

379 PAGES. 6x9 PAPERBACK. ILLUSTRATED. FOOTNOTES & BIBLIOGRAPHY. $14.95. CODE: LEM

LOST CITIES & ANCIENT MYSTERIES OF THE SOUTHWEST
By David Hatcher Childress

Join David as he starts in northern Mexico and searches for the lost mines of the Aztecs. He continues north to west Texas, delving into the mysteries of Big Bend, including mysterious Phoenician tablets discovered there and the strange lights of Marfa. Then into New Mexico where he stumbles upon a hollow mountain with a billion dollars of gold bars hidden deep inside it! In Arizona he investigates tales of Egyptian catacombs in the Grand Canyon, cruises along the Devil's Highway, and tackles the century-old mystery of the Lost Dutchman mine. In Nevada and California Childress checks out the rumors of mummified giants and weird tunnels in Death Valley, plus he searches the Mohave Desert for the mysterious remains of ancient dwellers alongside lakes that dried up tens of thousands of years ago. It's a full-tilt blast down the back roads of the Southwest in search of the weird and wondrous mysteries of the past!
486 Pages. 6x9 Paperback. Illustrated. $19.95. Code: LCSW

TECHNOLOGY OF THE GODS
The Incredible Sciences of the Ancients
by David Hatcher Childress

Childress looks at the technology that was allegedly used in Atlantis and the theory that the Great Pyramid of Egypt was originally a gigantic power station. He examines tales of ancient flight and the technology that it involved; how the ancients used electricity; megalithic building techniques; the use of crystal lenses and the fire from the gods; evidence of various high tech weapons in the past, including atomic weapons; ancient metallurgy and heavy machinery; the role of modern inventors such as Nikola Tesla in bringing ancient technology back into modern use; impossible artifacts; and more.
356 PAGES. 6x9 PAPERBACK. ILLUSTRATED. BIBLIOGRAPHY. $16.95. CODE: TGOD

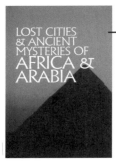

LOST CONTINENTS & THE HOLLOW EARTH
I Remember Lemuria and the Shaver Mystery
by David Hatcher Childress & Richard Shaver

Shaver's rare 1948 book *I Remember Lemuria* is reprinted in its entirety, and the book is packed with illustrations from Ray Palmer's *Amazing Stories* magazine of the 1940s. Palmer and Shaver told of tunnels running through the earth—tunnels inhabited by the Deros and Teros, humanoids from an ancient spacefaring race that had inhabited the earth, eventually going underground, hundreds of thousands of years ago. Childress discusses the famous hollow earth books and delves deep into whatever reality may be behind the stories of tunnels in the earth. Operation High Jump to Antarctica in 1947 and Admiral Byrd's bizarre statements, tunnel systems in South America and Tibet, the underground world of Agartha, the belief of UFOs coming from the South Pole, more.
344 PAGES. 6x9 PAPERBACK. ILLUSTRATED. $16.95. CODE: LCHE

LOST CITIES & ANCIENT MYSTERIES OF AFRICA & ARABIA
by David Hatcher Childress

Childress continues his world-wide quest for lost cities and ancient mysteries. Join him as he discovers forbidden cities in the Empty Quarter of Arabia; "Atlantean" ruins in Egypt and the Kalahari desert; a mysterious, ancient empire in the Sahara; and more. This is the tale of an extraordinary life on the road: across war-torn countries, Childress searches for King Solomon's Mines, living dinosaurs, the Ark of the Covenant and the solutions to some of the fantastic mysteries of the past.
423 PAGES. 6x9 PAPERBACK. ILLUSTRATED. $14.95. CODE: AFA

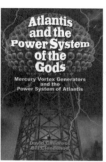

ATLANTIS & THE POWER SYSTEM OF THE GODS
by David Hatcher Childress and Bill Clendenon
Childress' fascinating analysis of Nikola Tesla's broadcast system in light of Edgar Cayce's "Terrible Crystal" and the obelisks of ancient Egypt and Ethiopia. Includes: Atlantis and its crystal power towers that broadcast energy; how these incredible power stations may still exist today; inventor Nikola Tesla's nearly identical system of power transmission; Mercury Proton Gyros and mercury vortex propulsion; more. Richly illustrated, and packed with evidence that Atlantis not only existed—it had a world-wide energy system more sophisticated than ours today.
246 PAGES. 6x9 PAPERBACK. ILLUSTRATED. $15.95. CODE: APSG

THE ANTI-GRAVITY HANDBOOK
edited by David Hatcher Childress
The new expanded compilation of material on Anti-Gravity, Free Energy, Flying Saucer Propulsion, UFOs, Suppressed Technology, NASA Cover-ups and more. Highly illustrated with patents, technical illustrations and photos. This revised and expanded edition has more material, including photos of Area 51, Nevada, the government's secret testing facility. This classic on weird science is back in a new format!
230 PAGES. 7x10 PAPERBACK. ILLUSTRATED. $16.95. CODE: AGH

ANTI-GRAVITY & THE WORLD GRID
Is the earth surrounded by an intricate electromagnetic grid network offering free energy? This compilation of material on ley lines and world power points contains chapters on the geography, mathematics, and light harmonics of the earth grid. Learn the purpose of ley lines and ancient megalithic structures located on the grid. Discover how the grid made the Philadelphia Experiment possible. Explore the Coral Castle and many other mysteries, including acoustic levitation, Tesla Shields and scalar wave weaponry. Browse through the section on anti-gravity patents, and research resources.
274 PAGES. 7x10 PAPERBACK. ILLUSTRATED. $14.95. CODE: AGW

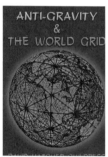

ANTI-GRAVITY & THE UNIFIED FIELD
edited by David Hatcher Childress
Is Einstein's Unified Field Theory the answer to all of our energy problems? Explored in this compilation of material is how gravity, electricity and magnetism manifest from a unified field around us. Why artificial gravity is possible; secrets of UFO propulsion; free energy; Nikola Tesla and anti-gravity airships of the 20s and 30s; flying saucers as superconducting whirls of plasma; anti-mass generators; vortex propulsion; suppressed technology; government cover-ups; gravitational pulse drive; spacecraft & more.
240 PAGES. 7x10 PAPERBACK. ILLUSTRATED. $14.95. CODE: AGU

THE TIME TRAVEL HANDBOOK
A Manual of Practical Teleportation & Time Travel
edited by David Hatcher Childress
The Time Travel Handbook takes the reader beyond the government experiments and deep into the uncharted territory of early time travellers such as Nikola Tesla and Guglielmo Marconi and their alleged time travel experiments, as well as the Wilson Brothers of EMI and their connection to the Philadelphia Experiment—the U.S. Navy's forays into invisibility, time travel, and teleportation. Childress looks into the claims of time travelling individuals, and investigates the unusual claim that the pyramids on Mars were built in the future and sent back in time. A highly visual, large format book, with patents, photos and schematics. Be the first on your block to build your own time travel device!
316 PAGES. 7x10 PAPERBACK. ILLUSTRATED. $16.95. CODE: TTH

MAPS OF THE ANCIENT SEA KINGS
Evidence of Advanced Civilization in the Ice Age
by Charles H. Hapgood
Charles Hapgood has found the evidence in the Piri Reis Map that shows Antarctica, the Hadji Ahmed map, the Oronteus Finaeus and other amazing maps. Hapgood concluded that these maps were made from more ancient maps from the various ancient archives around the world, now lost. Not only were these unknown people more advanced in mapmaking than any people prior to the 18th century, it appears they mapped all the continents. The Americas were mapped thousands of years before Columbus. Antarctica was mapped when its coasts were free of ice!

316 PAGES. 7x10 PAPERBACK. ILLUSTRATED. BIBLIOGRAPHY & INDEX. $19.95. CODE: MASK

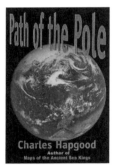

PATH OF THE POLE
Cataclysmic Pole Shift Geology
by Charles H. Hapgood
Maps of the Ancient Sea Kings author Hapgood's classic book *Path of the Pole* is back in print! Hapgood researched Antarctica, ancient maps and the geological record to conclude that the Earth's crust has slipped on the inner core many times in the past, changing the position of the pole. *Path of the Pole* discusses the various "pole shifts" in Earth's past, giving evidence for each one, and moves on to possible future pole shifts.

356 PAGES. 6x9 PAPERBACK. ILLUSTRATED. $16.95. CODE: POP

SECRETS OF THE HOLY LANCE
The Spear of Destiny in History & Legend
by Jerry E. Smith
Secrets of the Holy Lance traces the Spear from its possession by Constantine, Rome's first Christian Caesar, to Charlemagne's claim that with it he ruled the Holy Roman Empire by Divine Right, and on through two thousand years of kings and emperors, until it came within Hitler's grasp—and beyond! Did it rest for a while in Antarctic ice? Is it now hidden in Europe, awaiting the next person to claim its awesome power? Neither debunking nor worshiping, *Secrets of the Holy Lance* seeks to pierce the veil of myth and mystery around the Spear. Mere belief that it was infused with magic by virtue of its shedding the Savior's blood has made men kings. But what if it's more? What are "the powers it serves"?

312 PAGES. 6x9 PAPERBACK. ILLUSTRATED. BIBLIOGRAPHY. $16.95. CODE: SOHL

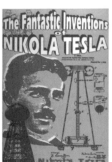

THE FANTASTIC INVENTIONS OF NIKOLA TESLA
by Nikola Tesla with additional material by
David Hatcher Childress
This book is a readable compendium of patents, diagrams, photos and explanations of the many incredible inventions of the originator of the modern era of electrification. In Tesla's own words are such topics as wireless transmission of power, death rays, and radio-controlled airships. In addition, rare material on a secret city built at a remote jungle site in South America by one of Tesla's students, Guglielmo Marconi. Marconi's secret group claims to have built flying saucers in the 1940s and to have gone to Mars in the early 1950s! Incredible photos of these Tesla craft are included. •His plan to transmit free electricity into the atmosphere. •How electrical devices would work using only small antennas. •Why unlimited power could be utilized anywhere on earth. •How radio and radar technology can be used as death-ray weapons in Star Wars.

342 PAGES. 6x9 PAPERBACK. ILLUSTRATED. $16.95. CODE: FINT

ROSWELL AND THE REICH
The Nazi Connection
By Joseph P. Farrell
Farrell has meticulously reviewed the best-known Roswell research from UFO-ET advocates and skeptics alike, as well as some little-known source material, and comes to a radically different scenario of what happened in Roswell, New Mexico in July 1947, and why the US military has continued to cover it up to this day. Farrell presents a fascinating case sure to disturb both ET believers and disbelievers, namely, that what crashed may have been representative of an independent postwar Nazi power—an extraterritorial Reich monitoring its old enemy, America, and the continuing development of the very technologies confiscated from Germany at the end of the War.

540 pages. 6x9 Paperback. Illustrated. $19.95. Code: RWR

SECRETS OF THE UNIFIED FIELD
The Philadelphia Experiment, the Nazi Bell, and the Discarded Theory
by Joseph P. Farrell
Farrell examines the now discarded Unified Field Theory. American and German wartime scientists and engineers determined that, while the theory was incomplete, it could nevertheless be engineered. Chapters include: The Meanings of "Torsion"; Wringing an Aluminum Can; The Mistake in Unified Field Theories and Their Discarding by Contemporary Physics; Three Routes to the Doomsday Weapon: Quantum Potential, Torsion, and Vortices; Tesla's Meeting with FDR; Arnold Sommerfeld and Electromagnetic Radar Stealth; Electromagnetic Phase Conjugations, Phase Conjugate Mirrors, and Templates; The Unified Field Theory, the Torsion Tensor, and Igor Witkowski's Idea of the Plasma Focus; tons more.

340 pages. 6x9 Paperback. Illustrated. $18.95. Code: SOUF

NAZI INTERNATIONAL
The Nazi's Postwar Plan to Control Finance, Conflict, Physics and Space
by Joseph P. Farrell
Farrell covers the vast, and still-little-known recreation of Nazi Germany in South America with help of Juan Peron, I.G. Farben and Martin Bormann. Farrell then covers Nazi Germany's penetration of the Muslim world including Wilhelm Voss and Otto Skorzeny in Gamel Abdul Nasser's Egypt before moving on to the development and control of new energy technologies including the Bariloche Fusion Project, Dr. Philo Farnsworth's Plasmator, and the work of Dr. Nikolai Kozyrev. Finally, Farrell discusses the Nazi desire to control space, and examines their connection with NASA, the esoteric meaning of NASA Mission Patches.

412 pages. 6x9 Paperback. Illustrated. $19.95. Code: NZIN

THE ILLUSTRATED DOOM SURVIVAL GUIDE
Don't Panic!
By Matt "DoomGuy" Victor
With over 500 very detailed and easy-to-understand illustrations, this book literally shows you how to do things like build a fire with whatever is at hand, perform field surgeries, identify and test foodstuffs, and form twine, snares and fishhooks. In any doomsday scenario, being able to provide things of real value—such as clothing, tools, medical supplies, labor, food and water—will be of the utmost importance. This book gives you the particulars to help you survive in any environment with little to no equipment, and make it through the first critical junctures after a disaster. Beyond any disaster you will have the knowledge to rebuild shelter, farm from seed to seed, raise animals, treat medical problems, predict the weather and protect your loved ones.

356 Pages. 6x9 Paperback. Illustrated. $20.00. Code: IDSG

ORDER FORM

One Adventure Place
P.O. Box 74
Kempton, Illinois 60946
United States of America
Tel.: 815-253-6390 • Fax: 815-253-6300
Email: auphq@frontiernet.net
http://www.adventuresunlimitedpress.com

ORDERING INSTRUCTIONS

✓ Remit by USD$ Check, Money Order or Credit Card

✓ Visa, Master Card, Discover & AmEx Accepted

✓ Paypal Payments Can Be Made To:

    info@wexclub.com

✓ Prices May Change Without Notice

✓ 10% Discount for 3 or More Items

SHIPPING CHARGES

United States

✓ Postal Book Rate { $4.50 First Item
50¢ Each Additional Item

✓ POSTAL BOOK RATE Cannot Be Tracked!
Not responsible for non-delivery.

✓ Priority Mail { $6.00 First Item
$2.00 Each Additional Item

✓ UPS { $7.00 First Item
$1.50 Each Additional Item

NOTE: UPS Delivery Available to Mainland USA Only

Canada

✓ Postal Air Mail { $15.00 First Item
$3.00 Each Additional Item

✓ Personal Checks or Bank Drafts MUST BE

US$ and Drawn on a US Bank

✓ Canadian Postal Money Orders OK

✓ Payment MUST BE US$

All Other Countries

✓ Sorry, No Surface Delivery!

✓ Postal Air Mail { $19.00 First Item
$7.00 Each Additional Item

✓ Checks and Money Orders MUST BE US$
and Drawn on a US Bank or branch.

✓ Paypal Payments Can Be Made in US$ To:
info@wexclub.com

SPECIAL NOTES

✓ RETAILERS: Standard Discounts Available

✓ BACKORDERS: We Backorder all Out-of-
Stock Items Unless Otherwise Requested

✓ PRO FORMA INVOICES: Available on Request

✓ DVD Return Policy: Replace defective DVDs only

ORDER ONLINE AT: www.adventuresunlimitedpress.com

**10% Discount When You Order
3 or More Items!**

Please check: ✓

☐ This is my first order   ☐ I have ordered before

Name

Address

City

State/Province   Postal Code

Country

Phone: Day   Evening

Fax   Email

Item Code	Item Description	Qty	Total

Please check: ✓

☐ Postal-Surface

☐ Postal-Air Mail
(Priority in USA)

☐ UPS
(Mainland USA only)

☐ Visa/MasterCard/Discover/American Express

Subtotal ▶	
Less Discount-10% for 3 or more items ▶	
Balance ▶	
Illinois Residents 6.25% Sales Tax ▶	
Previous Credit ▶	
Shipping ▶	
Total (check/MO in USD$ only) ▶	

Card Number:

Expiration Date: Security Code:

☐ SEND A CATALOG TO A FRIEND: